KAPLAN

Other Kaplan Books for College-Bound Students

College Admissions and Financial Aid

Straight Talk on Paying for College

Parent's Guide to College Admissions

The *Yale Daily News* Guide to Succeeding in College

Test Preparation

SAT Vocabulary Words Flip-O-Matic

SAT Math Mania

SAT

SAT Verbal Workbook

SAT Math Workbook

The Ring of McAllister

KAPLAN

SAT Vocabulary Flashcards

Extreme Flip-O-Matic

By the Staff of Kaplan, Inc.

Simon & Schuster

New York · London · Singapore · Sydney · Toronto

Kaplan Publishing
Published by Simon & Schuster
1230 Avenue of the Americas
New York, NY 10020

Contributing Editors: Seppy Basili and John Zeitlin
Project Editors: Ruth Baygell and Angela Cress
Interior Page Layout: Dave Chipps
Cover Design: Cheung Tai
Production Manager: Michael Shevlin
Editorial Coordinator: Déa Alessandro
Executive Editor: Del Franz

December 2003
10 9 8 7 6 5 4 3 2 1
Manufactured in the United States of America
Published simultaneously in Canada

ISBN 0-7432-5130-X

HOW TO USE THIS BOOK

More advanced than *Kaplan's SAT Vocabulary Words Flip-O-Matic*, *Kaplan's SAT Vocabulary Words Extreme Flip-O-Matic* is perfectly designed to help you learn 500 of the hardest essential SAT vocabulary words in a quick, easy, and fun way. Simply read the vocabulary word on the front of the flashcard and then flip to the back to see its definition, synonyms, and an example sentence with the SAT word in action. This amazing product conveniently allows you to skip over words once you've mastered them. All you have to do is clip or fold back the corner of the flashcard so that you can flip right by it on your next pass through the book. The *Extreme Flip-O-Matic* is packed with the toughest SAT vocabulary so you can flip your way to a higher score. Don't forget to flip the book over for the other half of the 500 hardest SAT words.

As a special bonus, we've included an SAT word root list at the back of this book for extra studying power. Grouping words together that share a common root meaning is a terrific and efficient way to familiarize yourself with strange or tough words you may encounter on the test.

Good luck, and happy flipping!

ABANDON

noun (uh baan duhn)

a gentle breeze; something airy or unsubstantial

The *zephyr* from the ocean made the intense heat on the beach bearable for the sunbathers.

synonyms: breath, draft

total lack of inhibition

With her strict parents out of town, Kelly danced all night with *abandon*.

synonyms: exuberance, enthusiasm

ZEPHYR

noun (zeh fuhr)

ABATE

verb (uh <u>bayt</u>)

the point of culmination; peak

The diva considered her appearance at the Metropolitan Opera to be the *zenith* of her career.

synonyms: acme, pinnacle

to decrease, to reduce

My hunger *abated* when I saw how filthy the chef's hands were.

synonyms: dwindle, ebb, recede

ZENITH

noun (zee nihth)

ABET

verb (uh beht)

a strong desire, craving

Pregnant women commonly have a *yen* for pickles.

synonyms: thirst, yearning

to aid; to act as an accomplice

While Derwin robbed the bank, Marvin *abetted* his friend by pulling up the getaway car.

synonyms: help, succor, assist

YEN

noun (yehn)

ABJURE

verb (aab <u>joor</u>)

bent or twisted in shape or condition; dryly humorous

Every time she teased him, she shot her friends a *wry* smile.

synonyms: askew, sardonic

to renounce under oath; to abandon forever; to abstain from

> After having been devout for most of his life, he suddenly *abjured* his beliefs, much to his family's disappointment.

synonyms: renounce, disavow

WRY

adj (rie)

ABNEGATE

verb (aab nih gayt)

to gain the advantage over; to defeat

The North *worsted* the South in America's Civil War.

synonyms: beat, vanquish

to give up; to deny to oneself

After his retirement, the former police commissioner found it difficult to *abnegate* authority.

synonyms: abjure, surrender, renounce

WORST

verb (wuhrst)

ABORTIVE

adj (uh <u>bohr</u> tihv)

charming, happily engaging

Dawn gave the customs officers a *winsome* smile, and they let her pass without searching her bags.

synonyms: attractive, delightful

ending without results

Her *abortive* attempt to swim the full five miles left her frustrated.

synonyms: fruitless, futile, unsuccessful

WINSOME

adj (wihn suhm)

ABROGATE

verb (<u>aab</u> ruh gayt)

---

clever; deceptive

Yet again, the *wily* coyote managed to elude the ranchers who wanted it dead.

synonyms: cunning, tricky, crafty

to annul; to abolish by authoritative action

The president's job is to *abrogate* any law that fosters inequality among citizens.

synonyms: nullify, revoke, repeal

WILY

adj (wie lee)

ABSCOND

verb (aab <u>skahnd</u>)

to exercise authority or influence effectively

For such a young congressman, he *wielded* a lot of power.

synonyms: exert, handle

to leave quickly in secret

The criminal *absconded* during the night with all of his mother's money.

synonyms: slip, sneak, flee

WIELD

verb (weeld)

ABSTEMIOUS

adj (aab stee mee uhs)

to increase gradually; to begin to be

The moon was *waxing*, and would soon be full.

synonyms: enlarge, expand

done sparingly; consuming in moderation

> The spa served no sugar or wheat, but the clients found the retreat so calm that they didn't mind the *abstemious* rules.

synonyms: moderate, sparing, abstinent

WAX

verb (waks)

ACCEDE

verb (aak <u>seed</u>)

undisciplined, unrestrained; reckless

The townspeople were outraged by the *wanton* display of disrespect when they discovered their statue of the town founder covered in graffiti.

synonyms: capricious, lewd, licentious

to express approval; to agree to

Once the mayor heard the reasonable request, she happily *acceded* to the proposal.

synonyms: consent, concur

WANTON

adj (wahn tuhn)

ACCLIVITY

noun (uh klihv ih tee)

sickly pale

The sick child had a *wan* face, in contrast to her rosy-cheeked sister.

synonyms: ashen, sickly

an incline or upward slope, the ascending side of a hill

> We were so tired from hiking that by the time we reached the *acclivity*, it looked more like a mountain than a hill.

synonyms: ascent, upgrade

WAN

adj (wahn)

ACCRETION

noun (uh kree shuhn)

talkative, speaking easily, glib

The *voluble* man and his reserved wife proved the old saying that opposites attract.

synonyms: loquacious, verbose

a growth in size; an increase in amount

> The committee's strong fund-raising efforts resulted in an *accretion* in scholarship money.

synonyms: buildup, accumulation

VOLUBLE

adj (vahl yuh buhl)

ACME

noun (aak mee)

a flight of missiles; round of gunshots

The troops fired a *volley* of bullets at the enemy, but they couldn't be sure how many hit their target.

synonyms: discharge, barrage

the highest level or degree attainable

Just when he reached the *acme* of his power, the dictator was overthrown.

synonyms: apex, peak, summit

VOLLEY

noun (vah lee)

ACTUATE

verb (<u>aak</u> choo ayt)

loud, noisy

Amid the *vociferous* protests of the members of parliament, the prime minister continued his speech.

synonyms: vocal, boisterous

to put into motion, to activate; to motivate or influence to activity

The leaders rousing speech *actuated* the crowd into a peaceful protest.

synonyms: incite, instigate

VOCIFEROUS

adj (voh sih fuhr uhs)

ACUITY

noun (uh kyoo ih tee)

to abuse verbally, berate

Vituperating someone is never a constructive way to effect change.

synonyms: scold, reproach, castigate

sharp vision or perception characterized by the ability to resolve fine detail

With unusual *acuity*, she was able to determine that the masterpiece was a fake.

synonyms: acuteness, sharpness

VITUPERATE

verb (vih too puhr ayt)

ACUMEN

noun (aak yuh muhn) (uh kyoo muhn)

instinctive, not intellectual; deep, emotional

When my twin was wounded many miles away, I, too, had a *visceral* reaction.

synonyms: gut, earthy

sharpness of insight, mind, and understanding; shrewd judgment

The investor's financial *acumen* helped him to select high-yield stocks.

synonyms: discernment, shrewdness

VISCERAL

adj (vihs uhr uhl)

ADAMANT

adj (aad uh muhnt) (aad uh mihnt)

extremely poisonous; malignant; hateful

Alarmed at the *virulent* press he was receiving, the militant activist decided to go underground.

synonyms: infectious, toxic

stubbornly unyielding

She was *adamant* about leaving the restaurant after the waiter was rude.

synonyms: inflexible, obdurate, inexorable

VIRULENT

adj (veer yuh luhnt)

ADEPT

adj (uh dehpt)

to clear of blame; support a claim

Tess felt *vindicated* when her prediction about the impending tornado came true.

synonyms: justify, exonerate

extremely skilled

She is *adept* at computing math problems in her head.

synonyms: quick, masterful

VINDICATE

verb (vihn dih kayt)

ADJUDICATE

verb (uh jood ih kayt)

vitality and energy

The *vim* with which she worked so early in the day explained why she was so productive.

synonyms: power, force

to hear and settle a matter; to act as a judge

The principal *adjudicated* the disagreement between two students.

synonyms: arbitrate, mediate

VIM

noun (vihm)

ADJURE

verb (uh joor)

to slander, defame

As gossip columnists often *vilify* celebrities, they're usually held in low regard.

synonyms: malign, slur

to appeal to

The criminal *adjured* to the court for mercy.

synonyms: beg, plead

VILIFY

verb (vih lih fie)

ADMONISH

verb (aad <u>mahn</u> ihsh)

felt or undergone as if one were taking part in the experience or feelings of another

She lived *vicariously* through the characters in the adventure books she was always reading.

synonyms: indirectly

to caution or warn gently in order to correct something

My mother *admonished* me about my poor grades.

synonyms: reprimand, rebuke

VICARIOUSLY

adverb (vie kaar ee uhs lee)

ADROIT

adj (uh <u>droyt</u>)

related to spring; fresh

Bea basked in the balmy *vernal* breezes, happy that winter was coming to an end.

synonyms: springlike, youthful

skillful; accomplished; highly competent

The *adroit* athlete completed even the most difficult obstacle course with ease.

synonyms: dexterous, proficient

VERNAL

adj (vuhr nuhl)

ADULATION

noun (aaj juh lay shuhn)

everyday language used by ordinary people; specialized language of a profession

Victor could not understand the *vernacular* of the south, where he had recently moved.

synonyms: dialect, patois, lingo

excessive flattery or admiration

The *adulation* she showed her professor seemed insincere; I suspected she really wanted a better grade.

synonyms: fawning, buttering up

VERNACULAR

noun (vuhr naa kyoo luhr)

ADUMBRATE

verb (<u>aad</u> uhm brayt) (uh <u>duhm</u> brayt)

being without question, often used figuratively

My neighbor was a *veritable* goldmine of information when I was writing my term paper on the Civil Rights era because she had been a student organizer and protester.

synonyms: authentic, bona fide

to give a hint or indication of something to come

Her constant complaining about the job *adumbrated* her intent to leave.

synonyms: foreshadow, suggest

VERITABLE

adj (vehr iht uh buhl)

AERIE

noun (ayr ee) (eer ee)

KAPLAN

wordy

The DNA analyst's answer was so *verbose* that the jury had trouble grasping his point.

synonyms: loquacious, garrulous

a nest built high in the air; an elevated, often secluded, dwelling

Perched high among the trees, the eagle's *aerie* was filled with eggs.

synonyms: perch, stronghold

VERBOSE

adj (vuhr bohs)

AFFECTED

adj (uh <u>fehk</u> tihd)

accuracy; truth

She had a reputation for *veracity*, so everyone believed her version of the story.

synonyms: truthfulness, reliability

phony, artificial

The *affected* hairdresser spouted French phrases, though she had never been to France.

synonyms: put-on, insincere, pretentious

VERACITY

noun (vuhr āā sih tee)

AGGREGATE

noun (aa grih giht)

marked by extreme intensity of emotions or convictions

She *vehemently* opposed the closing of the neighborhood garden, and was even arrested for protesting when the bulldozers came.

synonyms: vociferously, unequivocally

a collective mass, the sum total

> An *aggregate* of panic-stricken customers mobbed the bank, demanding their life savings.

synonyms: whole, entirety

VEHEMENTLY

adverb (vee uh muhnt lee)

ALGORITHM

noun (aal guh rith uhm)

varied; marked with different colors

The *variegated* foliage of the jungle allows it to support thousands of animal species.

synonyms: diversified

an established procedure for solving a problem or equation

> The accountant uses a series of *algorithms* to determine the appropriate tax bracket.

synonyms: calculation

VARIEGATED

adj (vaar ee uh gayt ehd)

ALIMENTARY

adj (aal uh <u>mehn</u> tuh ree) (aal uh <u>mehn</u> tree)

KAPLAN

the practice of lending money at exorbitant rates

The moneylender was convicted of *usury* when it was discovered that he charged 50 percent interest on all his loans.

synonyms: loan-sharking, interest

pertaining to food, nutrition, or digestion

> After a particularly good meal, Sherlock turned to his companion and exclaimed, “I feel quite good, very well fed. It was *alimentary* my dear Watson.”

synonyms: nourishing, nutritive

USURY

noun (yōō zhuh ree)

ALLAY

verb (uh <u>lay</u>)

to dethrone, especially of priestly power

Any priest caught sullying the good name of his profession would certainly be *unfrocked.*

synonyms: demote, degrade

to lessen, ease, reduce in intensity

Trying to *allay* their fears, the nurse sat with them all night.

synonyms: alleviate, soothe

UNFROCK

verb (uhn frahk)

AMITY

noun (aa mih tee)

unscrupulous; shockingly unfair or unjust

After she promised me the project, the fact that she gave it to someone else is *unconscionable.*

synonyms: dishonorable, indefensible

friendship, good will

Correspondence over the years contributed to a lasting *amity* between the women.

synonyms: harmony, benevolence

UNCONSCIONABLE

adj (uhn kahn shuhn uh buhl)

AMORPHOUS

adj (ay mohr fuhs)

so keen and perceptive as to seem supernatural, peculiarly unsettling

Though they weren't related, their resemblance was *uncanny*.

synonyms: weird, eerie

having no definite form

The Blob featured an *amorphous* creature that was constantly changing shape.

synonyms: shapeless, indistinct

UNCANNY

adj (uhn kaa nee)

ANIMUS

noun (<u>aan</u> uh muhs)

guardianship, guidance

Under the *tutelage* of her older sister, the young orphan was able to persevere.

synonyms: supervision

a feeling of animosity or ill will

Though her teacher had failed her, she displayed no *animus* toward him.

synonyms: hostility, animosity

TUTELAGE

noun (t$\overline{oo}$t uh lihj)

ANODYNE

noun (aan uh dyen)

swollen as from a fluid, bloated

In the process of osmosis, water passes through the walls of *turgid* cells, ensuring that they never contain too much water.

synonyms: distended

a source of comfort; a medicine that relieves pain

The sound of classical music is usually just the *anodyne* I need after a tough day at work.

synonyms: analgesic, painkiller

TURGID

adj (tuhr jihd)

ANOMALY

noun (uh nahm uh lee)

disposed to fight, belligerent

The bully was initially *truculent* but eventually stopped picking fights at the least provocation.

synonyms: antagonistic, combative

a deviation from the common rule, something that is difficult to classify

> Among the top-ten albums of the year was one *anomaly*—a compilation of polka classics.

synonyms: irregularity

TRUCULENT

adj (truhk yuh lehnt)

ANTHROPOMORPHIC

adj (aan thruh poh mohr fihk)

to beat severely, defeat

The inexperienced young boxer was *trounced* in a matter of minutes.

synonyms: vanquish, conquer

suggesting human characteristics for animals and inanimate things

> Many children's stories feature *anthropomorphic* animals such as talking wolves and pigs.

synonyms: humanlike

TROUNCE

verb (trowns)

ANTIQUATED

adj (<u>aan</u> tih kway tihd)

trembling, timid; easily shaken

The *tremulous* kitten had been separated from her mother.

synonyms: shaking, timorous, anxious

too old to be fashionable or useful

Next to her coworker's brand-new model, Marisa's computer looked *antiquated.*

synonyms: outdated, obsolete

TREMULOUS

adj (treh myoo luhs)

APHORISM

noun (<u>aa</u> fuhr ihz uhm)

---

short-lived, existing only briefly

The actress' popularity proved *transitory* when her play folded within the month.

synonyms: transient, ephemeral, momentary

a short statement of a principle

The country doctor was given to such *aphorisms* as “Still waters run deep.”

synonyms: adage, proverb

TRANSITORY

adj (traan sih tohr ee)

APLOMB

noun (uh <u>plahm</u>) (uh <u>pluhm</u>)

passing with time, temporary; short-lived

The reporter lived a *transient* life, staying in one place only long enough to cover the current story.

synonyms: brief, transitory

self-confident assurance; poise

> For such a young dancer, she had great *aplomb*, making her perfect to play the young princess.

synonyms: coolness, composure

TRANSIENT

adj (traan see uhnt)

APOSTATE

noun (uh pahs tayt)

synonyms: path, route, course

The *trajectory* of the pitched ball was interrupted by an unexpected bird.

the path followed by a moving object, whether through space or otherwise; flight

one who renounces a religious faith

> So that he could divorce his wife, the king scoffed at the church doctrines and declared himself an *apostate*.

synonyms: traitor, defector, deserter

TRAJECTORY

noun (truh jehk tuh ree)

APPOSITE

adj (<u>aap</u> puh ziht)

to praise or publicize loudly or extravagantly

She *touted* her skills as superior to ours, though in fact, we were all at the same level.

synonyms: acclaim, proclaim

strikingly appropriate or well adapted

> The lawyer presented an *apposite* argument upon cross-examining the star witness.

synonyms: apt, relevant, suitable

TOUT

verb (towt)

APPRISE

verb (uh priez)

having many twists and turns; highly complex

To reach the remote inn, the travelers had to negotiate a *tortuous* path.

synonyms: winding, circuitous

to give notice to, inform

"Thanks for *apprising* me that the test time has been changed," said Emanuel.

synonyms: notify

TORTUOUS

adj (tohr choo uhs)

APPROPRIATE

verb (uh proh pree ayt)

one who flatters in the hope of gaining favors

The king was surrounded by *toadies* who rushed to agree with whatever outrageous thing he said.

synonyms: sycophant, parasite

to assign to a particular purpose, allocate

The mayor *appropriated* funds for the clean-up effort.

synonyms: appoint, earmark

TOADY

noun (tōh dee)

ARABLE

adj (aa ruh buhl)

existing in title only; having a title without the functions or responsibilities

His prestige was merely a result of his *titular* rank, as he had no real power.

synonyms: honorary, named

suitable for cultivation

The overpopulated country desperately needed more *arable* land.

synonyms: farmable, fertile

TITULAR

adj (tich yoo luhr)

ARCANE

adj (ahr <u>kayn</u>)

to block or prevent from happening; frustrate, defeat the hopes or aspirations of

Thwarted in its attempt to get at the bananas inside the box, the chimp began to squeal.

synonyms: oppose, foil, frustrate

secret, obscure; known only to a few

The *arcane* rituals of the sect were passed down through many generations.

synonyms: esoteric, mysterious

THWART

verb (thwahrt)

ARCHIPELAGO

noun (ahr kuh <u>pehl</u> uh goh)

concise, brief, free of extra words

Her *terse* style of writing was widely praised by the editors, who had been used to seeing long-winded material.

synonyms: succinct, brusque

a large group of islands

Between villages in the Stockholm *archipelago*, boat taxis are the only form of transportation.

synonyms: cluster, scattering

TERSE

adj (tuhrs)

having little substance or strength; flimsy, weak

Francine's already *tenuous* connection to her cousins was broken when they moved away and left no forwarding address.

synonyms: thin, shaky

ARREARS

noun (uh <u>reerz</u>)

unpaid, overdue debts or bills; neglected obligations

After the expensive lawsuit, Dominic's accounts were in *arrears*.

synonyms: balance due

TENUOUS

adj (tehn yoo uhs)

ARROGATE

verb (aa ruh gayt)

a principle, belief, or doctrine accepted by members of a group

One of the *tenets* of Islam is that it is not acceptable to eat pork.

synonyms: canon

to claim without justification; to claim for oneself without right

> Lynn watched in astonishment as her boss *arrogated* the credit for her brilliant work on the project.

synonyms: take, presume, appropriate

TENET

noun (teh niht)

ASKANCE

adv (uh <u>skaans</u>)

tending to persist or cling; persistent in adhering to something valued or habitual

For years, against all odds, women *tenaciously* fought for the right to vote.

synonyms: stubborn, dogged, obstinate

with disapproval; with a skeptical sideways glance

She looked *askance* at her son's failing report card as he mumbled that he had done all the schoolwork.

synonyms: suspiciously

TENACIOUS

adj (tuh nay shuhs)

ASSENT

verb (uh sehnt)

having to do with, or limited by time

The story lacked a sense of the *temporal*, so we couldn't figure out if the events took place in one evening or over the course of a year.

synonyms: chronological, passing, ephemeral

to agree, as to a proposal

After careful deliberation, the CEO *assented* to the proposed merger.

synonyms: accede, yield, concur

TEMPORAL

adj (tehm puhr uhl) (tehm pruhl)

ATAVISTIC

adj (aat uh vihs tik)

stormy, turbulent

Our camping trip was cut short when the sun shower we were expecting turned into a *tempestuous* downpour.

synonyms: tumultuous, blustery

characteristic of a former era, ancient

After spending three weeks on a desert island, Roger became a survivalist with *atavistic* skills that helped him endure.

synonyms: old-fashioned, outdated

TEMPESTUOUS

adj (tehm pehs choo uhs)

AUTOCRAT

noun (<u>aw</u> toh kraat)

unreasonable or foolhardy disregard for danger, recklessness

I offered her a ride since it was late at night, but she had the *temerity* to say she'd rather walk.

synonyms: boldness

a dictator

Mussolini has been described as an *autocrat* who tolerated no opposition.

synonyms: tyrant, despot

KAPLAN

TEMERITY

noun (teh mehr ih tee)

AVER

verb (uh vuhr)

gaudy, cheap, showy

The performer changed into her *tawdry* costume and stepped onto the stage.

synonyms: flashy, chintzy

to declare to be true, to affirm

"Yes, he was holding a gun," the witness *averred*.

synonyms: assert, attest

TAWDRY

adj (taw dree)

AVUNCULAR

adj (ah vuhng kyuh luhr)

having to do with needless repetition, redundancy

I know he was only trying to clarify things, but his *tautological* statements confused me even more.

synonyms: verbose, wordy

like an uncle in behavior, especially in kindness and warmth

The coach's *avuncular* style made him well-liked.

TAUTOLOGICAL

adj (tawt uh lah jih kuhl)

AWRY

adv (uh rie)

equal in value or effect

If she didn't get concert tickets to see her favorite band, it would be *tantamount* to a tragedy.

synonyms: parallel, synonymous, equivalent

crooked, askew, amiss

> Something must have gone *awry* in the computer system because some of my files are missing.

synonyms: aslant, wrong

TANTAMOUNT

adj (taan tuh mownt)

producing a sensation of touch

The Museum of Natural History displays objects for people to touch so that they have a *tactile* understanding of how different peoples and animals lived.

synonyms: perceptible, tangible

BALK

verb (bawk)

to stop short and refuse to go on

> When the horse *balked* at jumping over the high fence, the rider was thrown off.

synonyms: flinch, shirk from

TACTILE

adj (taak tuhl) (taak tiel)

BALLAST

noun (baal uhst)

a person devoted to pleasure and luxury

A confirmed *sybarite*, the nobleman fainted at the thought of having to leave his palace and live in a small cottage.

synonyms: sensualist, voluptuary

a structure that helps to stabilize or steady

Communication and honesty are the true *ballasts* of a good relationship.

synonyms: counterweight, balancer

SYBARITE

noun (sih buh riet)

BEATIFIC

adj (bee uh <u>tihf</u> ihk)

to conquer, overcome

The blind woman *surmounted* great obstacles to become a well-known trial lawyer.

synonyms: clear, hurdle, leap

displaying calmness and joy, relating to a state of celestial happiness

After spending three months in India, she had a *beatific* peace about her.

synonyms: angelic, blissful

SURMOUNT

verb (suhr mownt)

BECALM

verb (bih <u>kahm</u>)

to replace (another) by force, to take the place of

The overthrow of the government meant a new leader to *supplant* the tyrannical former one.

synonyms: displace, supersede

to stop the progress of, to soothe

The warm air *becalmed* the choppy waves.

synonyms: quiet, allay, still

SUPPLANT

verb (suh plaant)

BECLOUD

verb (bih <u>klowd</u>)

to cause to be set aside; to force out of use as inferior, replace

Her computer was still running version 2.0 of the software, which had long since been *superseded* by at least three more versions.

synonyms: supplant, displace

to make less visible, obscure, or blur

> Her ambivalence about the long commute *beclouded* her enthusiasm about the job.

synonyms: muddle, cloud

SUPERSEDE

verb (soo puhr seed)

BEDRAGGLED

adj (bih <u>draag</u> uhld)

extra, more than necessary

The extra recommendations Jake included in his application were *superfluous*, as only one was required.

synonyms: excess, surplus

soiled, wet and limp; dilapidated

The child's *bedraggled* blanket needed a good cleaning.

synonyms: dishevelled, disordered, threadbare

SUPERFLUOUS

adj (soo puhr floo uhs)

BEGET

verb (bih <u>geht</u>)

KAPLAN

synonyms: defile, besmirch

With the help of a public-relations firm, he was able to restore his *sullied* reputation.

to tarnish, taint

to produce, especially as an effect or outgrowth; to bring about

> The mayor believed that finding petty offenders would help reduce serious crime because, he argued, small crimes *beget* big crimes.

synonyms: cause, breed

SULLY

verb (suh lee)

BEHEMOTH

noun (buh hee muhth)

hidden, secret; underground

Subterranean tracks were created for the trains after it was decided they had run out of room above ground.

synonyms: buried, concealed, sunken

something of monstrous size or power; huge creature

> The budget became such a *behemoth* that observers believed the film would never make a profit.

synonyms: giant, mammoth

SUBTERRANEAN

adj (suhb tuh rāy nee uhn)

BENEFICENT

adj (buh <u>nehf</u> ih suhnt)

to block or thwart

The police effort to capture the bank robber was *stymied* when he escaped through a rear window.

synonyms: stump, baffle, foil

pertaining to an act of kindness

The *beneficent* man donated the money anonymously.

synonyms: charitable, generous

STYMIE

verb (stie mee)

BERATE

verb (bih <u>rayt</u>)

imposing severe, rigorous standards

Many people found it difficult to live up to the *stringent* moral standards imposed by the Puritans.

synonyms: restricted, tight, demanding

to scold harshly

When my manager found out I had handled the situation so insensitively, he *berated* me.

synonyms: criticize, scold

STRINGENT

adj (strihn guhnt)

BILIOUS

adj (bihl yuhs)

loud, harsh, unpleasantly noisy

The traveler's *strident* manner annoyed the flight attendant, but she managed to keep her cool.

synonyms: grating, shrill, discordant

ill-tempered; sickly, ailing

> The party ended early when the *bilious* 5-year-old tried to run off with the birthday's girl's presents.

synonyms: pale, feeble, peevish

STRIDENT

adj (strie dehnt)

BLASPHEMOUS

adj (blaas fuh muhs)

to arrange or divide into layers

Schliemann *stratified* the numerous layers of Troy, an archeological dig that remains legendary.

synonyms: grade, separate

cursing, profane; extremely irreverent

The politician's offhanded biblical references seemed *blasphemous*, given the context of the orderly meeting.

synonyms: impious, profane, sacrilegious

STRATIFY

verb (straa tuh fie)

BLATANT

adj (blay tnt)

to specify as a condition or requirement of an agreement or offer

The contract *stipulated* that if the movie was never filmed, the actress got paid anyway.

synonyms: specifize, detail, designate

completely obvious and conspicuous, especially in an offensive, crass manner

> Such *blatant* advertising with the bounds of the school drew protest from parents.

synonyms: obvious, flagrant

KAPLAN

STIPULATE

verb (stihp yuh layt)

BLITHELY

adv (blieth lee)

to be sparing or frugal; to restrict with respect to a share or allowance

Don't *stint* on the mayonnaise, because I don't like my sandwich too dry.

synonyms: skimp, scrimp

merrily, lightheartedly cheerful; without appropriate thought

> Wanting to redecorate the office, she *blithely* assumed her co-workers wouldn't mind and moved the furniture in the space.

synonyms: in a carefree manner

STINT

verb (stihnt)

BOMBASTIC

adj (bahm baast ihk)

a state of static balance or equilibrium; stagnation

The rusty, ivy-covered World War II tank had obviously been in *stasis* for years.

synonyms: inertia, standstill

high-sounding but meaningless; ostentatiously lofty in style

> Mussolini's speeches were mostly *bombastic*; his outrageous claims had no basis in fact.

synonyms: grandiose, inflated

STASIS

noun (stay sihs)

BOVINE

adj (boh vien)

marked by outstanding strength and vigor of body, mind, or spirit

The 85-year old went to the market every day, impressing her neighbors with her *stalwart* routine.

synonyms: strong, bold

relating to cows; having qualities characteristic of a cow, such as sluggishness or dullness

His *bovine* demeanor did nothing to engage me.

synonyms: dull, placid

STALWART

adj (stahl wuhrt)

BRAGGART

noun (braag uhrt)

filthy and degraded as the result of neglect or poverty

The *squalid* living conditions in the building outraged the new tenants.

synonyms: unclean, foul

a person who brags or boasts in a loud and empty manner

Usually the biggest *braggart* at the company party, Susan's boss was unusually quiet at this year's event.

synonyms: boaster, showoff

SQUALID

adj (skwa lihd)

BROACH

verb (brohch)

frolicsome, playful

The lakeside vacation meant more *sportive* opportunities for the kids than the wine tour through France.

synonyms: frisky, merry

to mention or suggest for the first time

> Sandy wanted to go to college away from home, but he didn't know how to *broach* the topic with his parents.

synonyms: introduce, propose

SPORTIVE

adj (spohr tihv)

BUCOLIC

adj (byoo kahl lihk)

having the ring of truth but actually being untrue; deceptively attractive

After I followed up with some research on the matter, I realized that the charismatic politician's argument had been *specious*.

synonyms: misleading, untrue, captious

pastoral, rural

My aunt likes the hustle and bustle of the city, but my uncle prefers a more *bucolic* setting.

synonyms: rustic, country

SPECIOUS

adj (spee shuhs)

BURNISH

verb (<u>buhr</u> nihsh)

highly self-disciplined; frugal, austere

When he was in training, the athlete preferred to live in a *spartan* room, so he could shut out all distractions.

synonyms: restrained, simple

to polish; to make smooth and bright

Mr. Frumpkin loved to stand in the sun and *burnish* his luxury car.

synonyms: shine, buff

SPARTAN

adj (spahr tihn)

BURSAR

noun (<u>buhr</u> suhr) (<u>buhr</u> sahr)

exhibiting great immaturity and lack of judgment

After Sean's *sophomoric* behavior, he was grounded for weeks.

synonyms: juvenile, immature

treasurer or keeper of funds

The *bursar* of the school was in charge of allocating all scholarship funds.

SOPHOMORIC

adj (sahf mohr ihk)

CACHE

noun (caash)

synonyms: considerate, careful

Overjoyed to see the pop idol in her very presence, the *solicitous* store owner stood ready to serve.

anxious, concerned; full of desire, eager

a hiding place; stockpile

It's good to have a *cache* where you can stash your cash.

synonyms: hoard, reserve

SOLICITOUS

adj (suh lih sih tuhs)

CACOPHONY

noun (kuh <u>kah</u> fuh nee)

a temporary stay, visit

After graduating from college, Iliani embarked on a *sojourn* to China.

synonyms: layover, stay, rest

a jarring, unpleasant noise

As I walked into the open-air market after my nap, a *cacophony* of sounds surrounded me.

synonyms: clatter, racket

SOJOURN

noun (soh juhrn)

CALUMNY

noun (<u>kaa</u> luhm nee)

a nickname

One of former president Ronald Reagan's *sobriquets* was *The Gipper.*

synonyms: alias, pseudonym

a false and malicious accusation; misrepresentation

> The unscrupulous politician used *calumny* to bring down his opponent in the senatorial race.

synonyms: libel, defamation, slander

SOBRIQUET

noun (sōh brih kay) (sōh brih keht)

CANTANKEROUS

adj (kaan taang kuhr uhs)

a well-paying job or office that requires little or no work

The corrupt mayor made sure to set up all his relatives in *sinecures* within the administration.

having a difficult, uncooperative, or stubborn disposition

> The most outwardly *cantankerous* man in the nursing home was surprisingly sweet and loving with his grandchildren.

synonyms: contentious, ornery

SINECURE

noun (sien ih kyoor)

CAPTIOUS

adj (<u>kaap</u> shuhs)

apelike; relating to apes

Early man was more *simian* in appearance than is modern man.

synonyms: anthropoid, primate

marked by the tendency to point out trivial faults; intended to confuse in an argument

I resent the way he asked that *captious* question.

synonyms: critical, censorious

SIMIAN

adj (sih mee uhn)

CATACLYSMIC

adj (kaat uh <u>klihz</u> mihk)

KAPLAN

synonyms: heavenly, cherubic

Selena's *seraphic* appearance belied her nasty, bitter personality.

angelic, sweet

severely destructive

By all appearances, the storm seemed *cataclysmic*, though it lasted only a short while.

synonyms: catastrophic, tragic

SERAPHIC

adj (seh rah fihk)

CATALYST

noun (<u>kaat</u> uhl ihst)

to set apart, seclude

When juries are *sequestered*, it can take days, even weeks, to come up with a verdict.

synonyms: segregate, isolate

something that provokes or speeds up significant change, especially without being affected by the consequences

Technology has been a *catalyst* for the expansion of alternative education, such as home schooling and online courses.

synonyms: accelerator

SEQUESTER

verb (suh kweh stuhr)

CAUCUS

noun (<u>kaw</u> kuhs)

influential in an original way, providing a basis for further development; creative

The scientist's discovery proved to be *seminal* in the area of quantum physics.

synonyms: original, generative

a closed committee within a political party; a private committee meeting

The president met with the delegated *caucus* to discuss the national crisis.

synonyms: assembly, convention

SEMINAL

adj (seh muhn uhl)

CAUSTIC

adj (kah stihk)

behavior that promotes rebellion or civil disorder against the state

Li was arrested for *sedition* after he gave a fiery speech in the main square.

synonyms: insurrection, conspiracy

biting, sarcastic

> Writer Dorothy Parker gained her reputation for *caustic* wit, and her tombstone is inscribed with a fittingly clever "Excuse my dust."

synonyms: sardonic, incisive

SEDITION

noun (seh dih shuhn)

CEDE

verb (seed)

not specifically pertaining to religion, relating to the world

Although his favorite book was the Bible, the archbishop also read *secular* works such as mysteries.

synonyms: temporal, material

to surrender possession of something

Argentina *ceded* the Falkland Islands to Britain after a brief war.

synonyms: resign, yield, relinquish

SECULAR

adj (s̄eh kyuh luhr)

CELERITY

noun (seh leh rih tee)

morally degraded, unpleasant

The tour guide avoided the *seamy* parts of town.

synonyms: sordid, sleazy

speed, haste

The celebrity ran past his fans with great *celerity*.

synonyms: swiftness, briskness

SEAMY

adj (see mee)

CENSORIOUS

adj (sehn sohr ee uhs)

acting in strict regard for what is considered proper; punctiliously exact

After the storm had destroyed their antique lamp, the Millers worked to repair it with *scrupulous* care.

synonyms: painstaking, meticulous

critical; tending to blame and condemn

Closed-minded people tend to be *censorious* of others.

synonyms: fault-finding

SCRUPULOUS

adj (skroop yuh luhs)

CERTITUDE

noun (suhr tih tood)

synonyms: scholar

The *savant* so impressed us with his knowledge that we asked him to come speak at our school.

a person of learning; especially one with knowledge in a special field

assurance, freedom from doubt

The witness' *certitude* about the night in question had a big impact on the jury.

synonyms: certainty, conviction

SAVANT

noun (suh vahnt)

CESSATION

noun (seh <u>say</u> shuhn)

cold and steady in mood, gloomy; slow to act

Her *saturnine* expression every day made her hard to be around.

synonyms: sullen, bitter

a temporary or complete halt

The *cessation* of hostilities ensured that soldiers were able to spend the holidays with their families.

synonyms: arrest, termination

SATURNINE

adj (saat uhr nien)

CHARY

adj (<u>chahr</u> ee)

to satisfy (as a need or desire) fully or to excess

After years of journeying around the world with nothing but backpacks, the friends had finally *satiated* their desire to travel.

synonyms: gorge

watchful, cautious; extremely shy

> Mindful of the fate of the Titanic, the captain was *chary* of navigating the iceberg-filled sea.

synonyms: wary, careful

SATIATE

verb (say shee ayt)

hypocritically devout; acting morally superior to another

The *sanctimonious* columnist turned out to have been hiding a gambling problem that cost his family everything.

synonyms: pious, self-righteous

CHIMERICAL

adj (kie mehr ih kuhl) (kie meer ih kuhl)

fanciful; imaginary, impossible

> The inventor's plans seemed *chimerical* to the conservative businessman from whom he was asking for financial support.

synonyms: illusory, unreal

SANCTIMONIOUS

adj (saangk tih moh nee uhs)

CIRCUITOUS

adj (suhr kyoo ih tuhs)

prominent, of notable significance

His most *salient* characteristic is his tendency to dominate every conversation.

synonyms: noticeable, marked, outstanding

indirect, roundabout

> The venue was only a short walk from the train station, but a roadblock meant I had to take a *circuitous* route.

synonyms: lengthy, devious

SALIENT

adj (sāy lee uhnt)

CIRCUMVENT

verb (suhr kuhm vehnt)

KAPLAN

appealing to sexual desire

His television character was wholesomely funny, so audiences who saw his stand-up comedy routine were shocked by how *salacious* his jokes were.

synonyms: lustful

to go around; avoid

> Laura was able to *circumvent* the hospital's regulations, slipping into her mother's room long after visiting hours were over.

synonyms: evade, sidestep

SALACIOUS

adj (suh lay shuhs)

CLOYING

adj (kloy ing)

impious, irreverent toward what is held to be sacred or holy

It's considered *sacrilegious* for one to enter a mosque wearing shoes.

synonyms: profane, blasphemous

sickly sweet; excessive

When Dave and Liz got together their *cloying* affection towards one another often made their friends ill.

synonyms: excessive, fulsome

SACRILEGIOUS

adj (saak rih lihj uhs)

COAGULATE

verb (koh aag yuh layt)

KAPLAN

excessively sweet or sentimental

Geoffrey's *saccharine* poems nauseated Lucy, and she wished he'd stop sending them.

synonyms: maudlin, fulsome

to clot; to cause to thicken

Hemophiliacs can bleed to death from a minor cut because their blood does not *coagulate*.

synonyms: jell, congeal

SACCHARINE

adj (saa kuh rihn)

COGENT

adj (<u>koh</u> juhnt)

an elevated platform for public speaking

Though she was terrified, the new member of the debate club approached the *rostrum* with poise.

synonyms: stage, podium

logically forceful; compelling, convincing

> Swayed by the *cogent* argument of the defense, the jury had no choice but to acquit the defendant.

synonyms: persuasive, winning

ROSTRUM

noun (rahs truhm)

COLLOQUIAL

adj (kuh loh kwee uhl)

abundant prevalent especially to an increasing degree; filled with

The essay was so *rife* with grammatical errors that it had to be rewritten.

synonyms: numerous, prevailing

characteristic of informal speech

The book was written in a *colloquial* style so it would be user-friendlier.

synonyms: conversational, idiomatic

RIFE

adj (rief)

COMMUTE

verb (kuh <u>myoot</u>)

the art of speaking or writing effectively; skill in the effective use of speech

Lincoln's talent for *rhetoric* was evident in his beautifully expressed Gettysburg Address.

synonyms: eloquence, articulateness

to change a penalty to a less severe one

> In exchange for cooperating with detectives on another case, the criminal had his charges *commuted.*

synonyms: exchange, mitigate

RHETORIC

noun (reh tuhr ihk)

COMPLACENT

adj (kuhm <u>play</u> sihnt)

to criticize with harsh language, verbally abuse

The artist's new installation was *reviled* by critics who weren't used to the departure from his usual work.

synonyms: vituperate, scold, assail

self-satisfied, smug

Alfred always shows a *complacent* smile whenever he wins the spelling bee.

synonyms: contented, unconcerned

REVILE

verb (rih viel)

COMPLIANT

adj (kuhm <u>plie</u> uhnt)

splendid, brilliant

The bride looked *resplendent* in her gown and sparkling tiara.

synonyms: dazzling, bright

submissive, yielding

The boss was unused to an assistant who spoke her mind, but he grew to respect the fact that she wasn't *compliant*.

synonyms: bending, malleable

RESPLENDENT

adj (rih splehn duhnt)

CONCOMITANT

adj (kuh <u>kahm</u> ih tuhnt)

marked by firm determination

Louise was *resolute:* She would get into medical school no matter what.

synonyms: firm, unwavering, intent

existing concurrently

A double-major was going to be difficult to pull off, especially since Lucy would have to juggle two papers and two exams *concomitantly*.

synonyms: coexistent, concurrent

RESOLUTE

adj (reh suh loot)

CONCORD

noun (<u>kahn</u> kohrd)

KAPLAN

able to recover quickly after illness or bad luck; able to bounce back to shape

Psychologists say that being *resilient* in life is one of the keys to success and happiness.

synonyms: flexible, elastic

agreement

The sisters are now in *concord* about the car they had to share.

synonyms: accord, concurrence

RESILIENT

adj (rih sihl yuhnt)

CONDOLE

verb (kuhn dohl)

to repeal, cancel

After the celebrity was involved in a scandal, the car company *rescinded* its offer of an endorsement contract.

synonyms: void, annul, revoke

to grieve; to express sympathy

My hamster died when I was in third grade, and my friends *condoled* with me and helped bury him in the yard.

synonyms: console, sympathize

RESCIND

verb (rih sihnd)

CONFLAGRATION

noun (kahn fluh gray shuhn)

synonyms: reciprocate, compensate

Thanks for offering to lend me $1,000, but I know I'll never be able to *requite* your generosity.

to return or repay

big, destructive fire

After the *conflagration* had finally died down, the city center was nothing but a mass of blackened embers.

synonyms: blaze, inferno

REQUITE

verb (rih kwiet)

CONFLUENCE

noun (kahn floo uhns)

KAPLAN

to criticize or correct, usually in a gentle manner

Mrs. Hernandez *reproved* her daughter for staying out late and not calling.

synonyms: rebuke, admonish, reprimand

the act of two things flowing together; the junction or meeting place where two things meet

At the political meeting, while planning a demonstration, there was a moving *confluence* of ideas between members.

synonyms: junction, merging

REPROVE

verb (rih proov)

CONSANGUINEOUS

adj (kahn saang gwihn ee uhs)

blameworthy, disreputable

Lowell was thrown out of the bar because of his *reprehensible* behavior toward the other patrons.

synonyms: culpable, deplorable

having the same lineage or ancestry; related by blood

> After having a strange feeling about our relationship for years, I found out that my best friend and I are *consanguineous*.

synonyms: kin, cognate

REPREHENSIBLE

adj (rehp ree hehn suh buhl)

CONSTERNATION

noun (kahn stuhr <u>nay</u> shuhn)

relaxation, leisure

After working hard every day in the busy city, Mike finds his *repose* on weekends playing golf with friends.

synonyms: calmness, tranquility

an intense state of fear or dismay

One would never think that a seasoned hunter would display such *consternation* when a grizzly bear lumbered too close to camp.

synonyms: cowardice, fear

REPOSE

noun (rih pohz)

CONSTITUENT

noun (kuhn stih choo uhnt)

abundantly supplied, complete

The gigantic supermarket was *replete* with consumer products of every kind.

synonyms: abounding, full

component, part; citizen, voter

A machine will not function properly if one of its *constituents* is defective.

synonyms: element, factor

REPLETE

adj (rih pleet)

payment for goods or services or to recompense for losses

You can't expect people to do this kind of boring work without some form of *remuneration.*

synonyms: recompense, pay

CONSTRAINT

noun (kuhn <u>straynt</u>)

something that restricts or confines within prescribed bounds

Given the *constraints* of the budget, it was impossible to accomplish my goals.

synonyms: limitation, check

REMUNERATION

noun (rih myoo nuh ray shuhn)

KAPLAN

CONTEMPTUOUS

adj (kuhn <u>tehmp</u> choo uhs)

a lessening of intensity or degree

The doctor told me that the disease had gone into *remission*.

synonyms: abatement, subsiding

scornful; expressing contempt

The diners were intimidated by the waiter's *contemptuous* manner.

synonyms: derisive, disdainful, supercilious

REMISSION

noun (rih mih shuhn)

CONTENTIOUS

adj (kuhn tehn shuhs)

---

to send into exile, banish; assign

Because he hadn't scored any goals during the season, Abe was *relegated* to the bench for the championship game.

synonyms: consign, classify, refer

quarrelsome, disagreeable, belligerent

The *contentious* gentleman in the bar ridiculed anything anyone said.

synonyms: argumentative, fractious, litigious

RELEGATE

verb (reh luh gayt)

CONTIGUOUS

adj (kuhn tihg yoo uhs)

KAPLAN

to contradict, discredit

She made such a persuasive argument that nobody could *refute* it.

synonyms: deny

sharing a boundary; neighboring

> The two houses had *contiguous* yards so the families shared the landscaping expenses.

synonyms: bordering, adjoining

REFUTE

verb (rih fyoot)

CONTINENCE

noun (kahn tih nihns)

to deflect sound or light

The crystal *refracted* the rays of sunlight so they formed a beautiful pattern on the wall.

synonyms: bend, slant

self-control, self-restraint

> Lucy exhibited impressive *continence* in steering clear of fattening foods, and she lost 50 pounds.

synonyms: moderation, discipline

REFRACT

verb (rih fraakt)

CONVALESCE

verb (kahn vuhl ehs)

a tendency to relapse into a previous behavior, especially criminal behavior

According to statistics, the *recidivism* rate for criminals is quite high.

synonyms: return, backslide, relapse

to gradually recover from an illness

After her bout with malaria, Tatiana needed to *convalesce* for a whole month.

synonyms: heal, recuperate

RECIDIVISM

noun (rih sihd uh vih zihm)

CONVERGENCE

noun (kuhn vuhr juhns)

to review by a brief summary

After the long-winded president had finished his speech, his assistant *recapitulated* for the press the points he had made.

synonyms: synopsize, condense, digest

the state of separate elements joining or coming together

A *convergence* of factors led to the tragic unfolding of World War I.

synonyms: union, concurrence, coincidence

RECAPITULATE

verb (ree kuh pihch yoo layt)

COQUETTE

noun (koh keht)

---

marked by extreme conservatism, especially in politics

The former radical hippie had turned into quite a *reactionary*, and the press tried to expose her as a hypocrite.

synonyms: ultraconservative, right-wing, orthodox

a flirtatious woman

The librarian could turn into a *coquette* just by letting her hair down and changing the swing of her hips.

synonyms: flirt

REACTIONARY

adj (ree aak shuhn ayr ee)

COTERIE

noun (koh tuh ree)

to tear down, demolish

The house had been *razed*; where it once stood, there was nothing but splinters and bricks.

synonyms: level, destroy

an intimate group of persons with a similar purpose

Judith invited a *coterie* of fellow stamp enthusiasts to a stamp-trading party.

synonyms: clique, set

RAZE

verb (rayz)

COUNTERVAIL

verb (<u>kown</u> tuhr vayl)

to make rare; to make thin or less dense

The atmosphere *rarefies* as altitude increases, so the air atop a mountain is too thin to breathe.

synonyms: attenuate, prune

to act or react with equal force

In order to *countervail* the financial loss the school suffered after the embezzlement, the treasurer raised the price of room and board.

synonyms: counteract, compensate, offset

RAREFY

verb (rayr uh fie)

COVERT

adj (koh vuhrt)

deeply absorbed

The story was so well performed that the usually rowdy children were *rapt* until the final word.

synonyms: engrossed, immersed

secretive, not openly shown

The *covert* military operation wasn't disclosed until weeks later after it was determined to be a success.

synonyms: veiled

RAPT

adj (raapt)

taking by force; driven by greed

Sea otters are so *rapacious* that they consume 10 times their body weight in food every day.

synonyms: ravenous, voracious

CULL

verb (kuhl)

to select, weed out

You should *cull* the words you need to study from all the flash cards.

synonyms: pick, extract

RAPACIOUS

adj (ruh pay shuhs)

CUMULATIVE

adj (kyoom yuh luh tihv)

to cause anger and irritation

At first the kid's singing was adorable, but after 40 minutes it began to *rankle*.

synonyms: embitter, annoy

increasing, collective

The new employee didn't mind her job at first, but the daily petty indignities had a *cumulative* demoralizing effect.

synonyms: added up, gradual

RANKLE

verb (raang kuhl)

CURT

adj (kuhrt)

bitter hatred

Having been teased mercilessly for years, Herb became filled with *rancor* toward those who had humiliated him.

synonyms: deep-seated ill will

abrupt, short with words

The grouchy shop assistant was *curt* with one of her customers, which resulted in a reprimand from her manager.

synonyms: terse, rude

RANCOR

noun (raan kuhr)

DEARTH

noun (duhrth)

to profess, suppose, claim

Brad *purported* to be an opera lover, but he fell asleep at every performance he attended.

synonyms: pretend, purpose

a lack, scarcity, insufficiency

The *dearth* of supplies in our city made it difficult to survive the blizzard.

synonyms: absence, shortage

PURPORT

verb (puhr pohrt)

DEBACLE

noun (dih <u>baa</u> kuhl)

to steal

The amateur detective Dupin found the *purloined* letter for which the police had searched in vain.

synonyms: pilfer, embezzle

a sudden, disastrous collapse or defeat; a total, ridiculous failure

> It was hard for her to show her face in the office after the *debacle* of spilling coffee on her supervisor—three times.

synonyms: crash, wreck

PURLOIN

verb (puhr loyn)

DECLAIM

verb (dih <u>klaym</u>)

one who gives opinions in an authoritative manner

The *pundits* on television are often more entertaining than the sitcoms.

synonyms: critic

to speak loudly and vehemently

At Thanksgiving dinner, our grandfather always *declaims* his right, as the eldest, to sit at the head of the table.

synonyms: perorate, rant, rave

PUNDIT

noun (puhn diht)

DEFAMATORY

adj (dih faam uh tohr ee)

concerned with precise details about codes or conventions

The *punctilious* student never made spelling errors on her essays.

synonyms: precise, scrupulous, meticulous

injurious to the reputation

The tabloid was sued for making *defamatory* statements about the celebrity.

synonyms: libelous, slanderous

PUNCTILIOUS

adj (puhngk tihl ee uhs)

DEMAGOGUE

noun (deh muh gahg) (deh muh gawg)

powerful

His memoir was full of descriptions of *puissant* military heroics, but most were exaggerations or outright lies.

synonyms: strong

leader, rabble-rouser, usually using appeals to emotion or prejudice

> Hitler began his political career as a *demagogue*, giving fiery speeches in beer halls.

synonyms: agitator, inciter, instigator

PUISSANT

adj (pwih siht) (pyoo siht)

DENIZEN

noun (<u>dehn</u> ih zuhn)

KAPLAN

boxing

Pugilism has been defended as a positive outlet for aggressive impulses.

synonyms: sparring, fighting

an inhabitant, a resident

The *denizens* of the state understandably wanted to select their own leaders.

synonyms: citizen, habitant, occupant

PUGILISM

noun (pyoo juhl ih suhm)

DERIDE

verb (dih ried)

a fictitious name, used particularly by writers to conceal identity

Though George Eliot sounds as though it's a male name, it was the *pseudonym* that Marian Evans used when she published her classic novel *Middlemarch*.

synonym: pen name

to laugh at contemptuously, to make fun of

As soon as George heard the others *deriding* Anthony, he came to his defense.

synonyms: ridicule

PSEUDONYM

noun (soo duh nihm)

DIFFUSE

verb (dih <u>fyooz</u>)

a person authorized to act for someone else

In the event the stock shareholder can't attend the meeting, he'll send a *proxy*.

synonym: representative, alternate

to spread out widely, to scatter freely, to disseminate

> They turned on the fan, but all that did was *diffuse* the cigarette smoke throughout the room.

synonyms: disperse, soften

PROXY

noun (prahk see)

DIGRESS

verb (die grehs)

limited in outlook, narrow, unsophisticated

Having grown up in the city, Anita sneered at the *provincial* attitudes of her country cousins.

synonyms: unpolished, unrefined

to turn aside, especially from the main point; to stray from the subject

The professor repeatedly *digressed* from the topic, boring his students.

synonyms: deviate, wander

PROVINCIAL

adj (pruh vihn shuhl)

DILAPIDATED

adj (dih laap ih dayt ihd)

synonyms: submissive

Lying *prostrate* awaiting the Pope, a car splashed me with water.

lying face downward in adoration or submission

in disrepair, run down

Rather than get discouraged, the architect saw great potential in the *dilapidated* house.

synonyms: decayed, fallen into partial ruin

PROSTRATE

adj (prah strayt)

DILUVIAL

adj (dih <u>loo</u> vee uhl)

to condemn or forbid as harmful or unlawful

Consumption of alcohol was *proscribed* in the country's constitution, but the ban was eventually lifted.

synonyms: prohibit, ban

pertaining to a flood

After she left the water running in the house all day, it looked simply *diluvial*.

synonyms: waterlogged

PROSCRIBE

verb (proh skrieb)

DISCOMFIT

verb (dihs kuhm fiht)

relating to prose (as opposed to poetry); dull, ordinary

Simon's *prosaic* style bored his writing teacher to tears, though he thought he had an artistic flair.

synonyms: unimaginative, everyday

to disconcert, to make one lose one's composure

The class clown enjoyed *discomfiting* her classmates whenever possible.

synonyms: embarrass, thwart the plans of

PROSAIC

adj (proh say ihk)

DISCRETE

adj (dih <u>skreet</u>)

A natural inclination or preference

She has a *propensity* for lashing out at others when stressed, so we leave her alone when she's had a rough day.

synonyms: tendency

individually distinct, separate

> What's nice about the CD is that each song functions as a *discrete* work and also as part of the whole compilation.

synonyms: unconnected, distinct

PROPENSITY

noun (proh pehn sih tee)

DISINGENUOUS

adj (dihs ihn jehn yoo uhs)

to make known by open declaration, proclaim

The publicist *promulgated* the idea that the celebrity had indeed gotten married.

synonyms: announce, broadcast

giving a false appearance of simple frankness; misleading

> It was *disingenuous* of him to suggest that he had no idea of the requests made by his campaign contributors.

synonyms: insincere, tricky

PROMULGATE

verb (prah muhl gayt)

DISINTERESTED

adj (dihs <u>ihn</u> trih stihd) (dihs <u>ihn</u> tuh reh stihd)

to grow by rapid production of new parts; increase in number

The cancer cells *proliferated* so quickly that even the doctor was surprised.

synonyms: multiply

fair-minded, unbiased

A fair trial is made possible by the selection of *disinterested* jurors.

synonyms: impartial, unprejudiced

PROLIFERATE

verb (proh lih fuhr ayt)

DISPASSIONATE

adj (dihs paash uh niht)

an ancestor in the direct line, forefather; founder

Though his parents had been born here, his *progenitors* were from India.

synonyms: inventor

unaffected by bias or strong emotions; not personally or emotionally involved in something

Ideally, photographers should be *dispassionate* observers of what goes on in the world.

synonyms: disinterested, impartial

PROGENITOR

noun (proh jehn ih tuhr)

DISSIDENT

adj (<u>dihs</u> ih duhnt)

to offer for acceptance

The deal *proffered* by the committee satisfied all those at the meeting, ending a month-long discussion.

synonyms: propose

disagreeing with an established religious or political system

The *dissident* had been living abroad and writing his criticism of the government from an undisclosed location.

synonyms: heretical

PROFFER

verb (prahf uhr)

DOCTRINAIRE

adj (dahk truh nayr)

recklessly extravagant, wasteful

The *prodigal* expenditures on the military budget during a time of peace created a stir in the Cabinet.

synonyms: lavish

rigidly devoted to theories without regard for practicality; dogmatic

The professor's manner of teaching was considered *doctrinaire* for such a liberal school.

synonyms: inflexible, dictatorial

PRODIGAL

adj (prah dih guhl)

DOGGED

adj (daw guhd)

ancient, primitive

The archaeologist claimed that the skeleton was of *primeval* origin, though in fact it was the remains of a modern-day monkey.

synonyms: primordial, original

stubbornly persevering

The police inspector's *dogged* determination helped him catch the thief.

synonyms: tenacious, obstinate

PRIMEVAL

adj (priem ee vuhl)

DOLEFUL

adj (dohl fuhl)

existing outside of nature; extraordinary; supernatural

We were all amazed at her *preternatural* ability to recall smells from her early childhood.

synonyms: psychic, abnormal

sad, mournful

Looking into the *doleful* eyes of the lonely pony, the girl yearned to take him home.

synonyms: dejected, woeful

PRETERNATURAL

adj (pree tuhr naach uhr uhl)

a cleverly executed trick or deception; sleight of hand

My hunch was that he won the contest not so much as a result of real talent, but rather through *prestidigitation*.

DOUR

adj (doo uhr) (dow uhr)

sullen and gloomy; stern and severe

The *dour* hotel concierge demanded payment for the room in advance.

synonyms: austere, strict, grave

PRESTIDIGITATION

noun (prehs tih dihj ih tay shuhn)

EFFLUVIA

noun (ih floo vee uh)

something that foreshadows; a feeling of what will happen in the future

The demolition of the Berlin Wall was a *presage* to the fall of the Soviet Union.

synonyms: premonition

waste; odorous fumes given off by waste

He took out the garbage at 3 A.M. because the *effluvia* had begun wafting into the bedroom.

synonyms: odor, stench

PRESAGE

noun (preh sihj)

ELEGY

noun (eh luh jee)

steeply; hastily

At the sight of the approaching helicopters, Private Johnson *precipitously* shot a flare into the air.

synonyms: impetuous, headlong, reckless

a mournful poem, usually about the dead

A memorable *elegy* was read aloud for the spiritual leader.

synonyms: memorial, lament

PRECIPITOUSLY

adv (prih sihp ih tuhs lee)

ELUDE

verb (ih lood)

lacking in security or stability; dependent on chance or uncertain conditions

Given the *precarious* circumstances, I chose to opt out of the deal completely.

synonyms: doubtful, chancy

to avoid cleverly, to escape the perception of

> Somehow, the runaway *eluded* detection for weeks.

synonyms: evade, dodge

PRECARIOUS

adj (prih caa ree uhs)

EMOLLIENT

adj (ih mohl yuhnt)

---

a ruler; one who wields great power

Alex was much kinder before he assumed the role of *potentate*.

synonyms: leader, dominator

soothing, especially to the skin

> After being out in the sun for so long, the *emollient* cream was a welcome relief on my skin.

synonyms: softening, mollifying

POTENTATE

noun (poh tehn tayt)

EMULATE

verb (ehm yuh layt)

suitable for drinking

Though the water was *potable*, it tasted terrible.

synonyms: unpolluted

to strive to equal or excel, to imitate

Children often *emulate* their parents.

synonyms: follow, mimic

POTABLE

adj (poh tuh buhl)

ENCUMBER

verb (ehn <u>kuhm</u> buhr)

to assume as real or conceded; propose as an explanation

Before proving the math formula, we needed to *posit* that *x* and *y* were real numbers.

synonyms: suggest

to weigh down, to burden

> She often felt *encumbered* by the distractions of the city, so she sought a quieter place in the country.

synonyms: hamper, oppress, saddle

POSIT

verb (pohz iht)

ENJOIN

verb (ehn joyn)

foreshadowing, ominous; eliciting amazement and wonder

Everyone thought the rays of light were *portentous* until they realized a nine-year-old was playing a joke on them.

synonyms: premonitory

to direct or impose with urgent appeal, to order with emphasis; to forbid

> Patel is *enjoined* by his culture from eating the flesh of a cow, which is sacred in India.

synonyms: instruct, charge

PORTENTOUS

adj (pohr tehn tuhs)

EPOCHAL

adj (ehp uh kuhl) (ehp ahk uhl)

to read studiously or attentively

I've *pored* over this text, yet I still can't understand it.

synonyms: stare, ponder

momentous, highly significant

The Supreme Court's *epochal* decision will no doubt affect generations to come.

synonyms: unparalleled, notable

PORE

verb (pohr)

EPONYMOUS

adj (ih pahn uh muhs)

a speaker of many languages

Ling's extensive travels have helped her to become a true *polyglot*.

giving one's name to a place, book, restaurant

Macbeth was the *eponymous* protagonist of Shakespeare's play.

synonyms: named after

POLYGLOT

noun (pah lee glaht)

EQUIVOCATE

verb (ih <u>kwihv</u> uh kayt)

synonyms: tactful

She was wise to curb her tongue and was able to explain her problem to the judge in a respectful and *politic* manner.

shrewd and crafty in managing or dealing with things

to avoid committing oneself in what one says, to be deliberately unclear

> Not wanting to implicate himself in the crime, the suspect *equivocated* for hours.

synonyms: lie, mislead

POLITIC

adj (pah lih tihk)

ERSATZ

adj (uhr sahtz)

---

courageous; spunky

The *plucky* young nurse dove into the foxhole, determined to help the wounded soldier.

synonyms: brave

being an artificial and inferior substitute or imitation

The *ersatz* strawberry shortcake tasted more like plastic than like real cake.

synonyms: fake, counterfeit

PLUCKY

adj (pluh kee)

ESCHEW

verb (ehs <u>choo</u>)

crude or coarse; characteristic of commoners

After five weeks of rigorous studying, the graduate settled in for a weekend of *plebeian* socializing and television watching.

synonyms: unrefined, conventional

to shun; to avoid (as something wrong or distasteful)

> The filmmaker *eschewed* artifical light for her actors, resulting in a stark movie style.

synonyms: evade, escape

PLEBEIAN

adj (plee bee uhn)

ESPOUSE

verb (ih <u>spowz</u>)

overused and trite remark

Instead of the usual *platitudes*, the comedian gave a memorable and inspiring speech to the graduating class.

synonyms: cliché

to take up and support as a cause; to marry

> Because of his religious beliefs, the preacher could not *espouse* the use of capital punishment.

synonyms: champion, adopt

PLATITUDE

noun (plaa tih tood)

ESPY

verb (ehs pie)

expressive of suffering or woe, melancholy

The *plaintive* cries from the girl trapped in the tree were heard by all.

synonyms: mournful, sorrowful

to catch sight of, glimpse

> Amidst a crowd in black clothing, she *espied* the colorful dress that her friend was wearing.

synonyms: discern

PLAINTIVE

adj (playn tihv)

EUPHEMISM

noun (<u>yoo</u> fuh mihz uhm)

to arouse anger or resentment in; provoke

His continual insensitivity *piqued* my anger.

synonyms: irritate, rouse

an inoffensive and agreeable expression that is substituted for one that is considered offensive

The funeral director preferred to use the *euphemism* "passed away" instead of the word "dead."

PIQUE

verb (peek)

having a sluggish, unemotional temperament

His writing was energetic but his *phlegmatic* personality wasn't suited for television, so he turned down the interview.

synonyms: matter-of-fact, undemonstrative

EUTHANASIA

noun (yoo thun nay zhuh)

the practice of ending the life of hopelessly ill individuals; assisted suicide

Euthanasia has always been the topic of much moral debate.

synonyms: mercy-killing

PHLEGMATIC

adj (flehg maa tihk)

EXCORIATE

verb (ehk skohr ee ayt)

the study of ancient texts and languages

Philology was the predecessor to modern-day linguistics.

to censure scathingly; to express strong disapproval of

The three-page letter to the editor *excoriated* the publication for printing the rumor without verifying the source.

synonyms: denounce

PHILOLOGY

noun (fih lahl uh jee)

EXPONENT

noun (<u>ehk</u> spoh nuhnt)

a person who is guided by materialism and is disdainful of intellectual or artistic values

The *philistine* never even glanced at the rare violin in his collection but instead kept an eye on its value and sold it at a profit.

one who champions or advocates

The vice president was an enthusiastic *exponent* of computer technology.

synonyms: supporter, representative

PHILISTINE

noun (fihl uh steen)

EXPOUND

verb (ihk spownd)

a compact or close-knit body of people, animals, or things

A *phalanx* of guards stood outside the prime minister's home day and night.

synonyms: mass, legion

to explain or describe in detail

The teacher *expounded* on the theory of relativity for hours.

synonyms: elucidate, elaborate

PHALANX

noun (fay laanks)

KAPLAN

EXPUNGE

verb (ihk spuhnj)

to travel on foot

It has always been a dream of mine to *peregrinate* from one side of Europe to the other with nothing but a backpack.

synonyms: walk, traverse

to erase, eliminate completely

> The parents' association *expunged* the questionable texts from the children's reading list.

synonyms: delete, obliterate

PEREGRINATE

verb (pehr ih gruh nayt)

EXTIRPATE

verb (ehk stuhr payt)

an oppressive lack of resources (as money), severe poverty

Once a famous actor, he eventually died in *penury* and anonymity.

synonyms: destitution, impoverishment

to root out, eradicate, literally or figuratively; to destroy wholly

The terrorist cells were *extirpated* after many years of investigation.

synonyms: wipe out

KAPLAN

PENURY

noun (pehn yuh ree)

EXTRAPOLATION

noun (ihk strap uh lay shuhn)

expressing sorrow for sins or offenses, repentant

Claiming the murderer did not feel *penitent*, the victim's family felt his pardon should be denied.

synonyms: remorseful, apologetic

the process of using known data and information to determine what will happen in the future

Through the process of *extrapolation*, we were able to determine which mutual funds to invest in.

synonyms: projection, forecast

PENITENT

adj (pehn ih tuhnt)

EXTRINSIC

adj (ihk strihn sihk) (ihk strihn zihk)

---

an inclination, a definite liking

After Daniel visited the Grand Canyon, he developed a *penchant* for travel.

synonyms: leaning, predilection

external, unessential; originating from the outside

> "Though they are interesting to note," the meeting manager claimed, "those facts are *extrinsic* to the matter under discussion."

synonyms: extraneous, foreign

PENCHANT

noun (pehn chuhnt)

EXTRUDE

verb (ihk <u>strood</u>)

transparently clear in style or meaning, easy to understand

Though she thought she could hide her ulterior motives, they were *pellucid* to everyone else.

synonyms: apparent

to form or shape something by pushing it out, to force out, especially through a small opening

We watched in awe as the volcano *extruded* molten lava.

synonyms: squeeze out

PELLUCID

adj (peh loo sihd)

FACETIOUS

adj (fuh <u>see</u> shuhs)

relating to money

Michelle's official title was office manager, but she ended up taking on a lot of *pecuniary* responsibilities such as payroll duties.

synonyms: fiscal, financial

witty, humorous

Her *facetious* remarks made the uninteresting meeting more lively.

synonyms: amusing, comical

PECUNIARY

adj (pih kyoon nee ehr ee)

FACILE

adj (faa suhl)

KAPLAN

to embezzle

These days in the news, we read more and more about workers *peculating* the system.

synonyms: misappropriate

easily accomplished; seeming to lack sincerity or depth; arrived at without due effort

Given the complexity of the problem, it seemed a rather *facile* solution.

synonyms: effortless, superficial

PECULATE

verb (pehk yuh layt)

FALLACIOUS

adj (fuh <u>lay</u> shuhs)

to act as patron of, to adopt an air of condescension toward; to buy from

LuAnn *patronized* the students, treating them like simpletons, which they deeply resented.

synonyms: condescend

tending to deceive or mislead; based on a fallacy

The *fallacious* statement "the Earth is flat" misled people for many years.

synonyms: false, erroneous

PATRONIZE

verb (pay truh niez)

FEBRILE

adj (<u>fehb</u> ruhl) (<u>fee</u> bruhl)

KAPLAN

aristocratic

Though he really couldn't afford an expensive lifestyle, Claudius had *patrician* tastes.

synonyms: high-class

feverish, marked by intense emotion or activity

Awaiting the mysterious announcement, there was a *febrile* excitement in the crowd.

synonyms: agitated, flushed

PATRICIAN

adj (puh trih shuhn)

causing disease

Bina's research on the origins of *pathogenic* microorganisms should help stop the spread of disease.

synonyms: noxious, infecting

FECKLESS

adj (<u>fehk</u> lihs)

ineffective, worthless

Anja took on the responsibility of caring for her aged mother, realizing that her *feckless* sister was not up to the task.

synonyms: incompetent

PATHOGENIC

adj (paa thuh jehn ihk)

FEIGN

verb (fayn)

obvious, evident

Moe could no longer stand Frank's *patent* fawning over the boss and so confronted him.

synonyms: unconcealed, clear

to pretend, to give a false appearance of

> Though she had discovered they were planning a party, she *feigned* surprise so as not to spoil the festivities.

synonyms: fake

PATENT

adj (paa tehnt)

FERAL

adj (fehr uhl)

an outcast

Once he betrayed those in his community, he was banished and lived the life of a *pariah*.

synonyms: untouchable, abomination

suggestive of a wild beast, not domesticated

> Though the animal-rights activists did not want to see the *feral* dogs harmed, they offered no solution to the problem.

synonyms: wild, savage

PARIAH

noun (puh rie ah)

FICTIVE

adj (<u>fihk</u> tihv)

KAPLAN

to trim off excess, reduce

The cook's hands were sore after she *pared* hundreds of potatoes for the banquet.

synonyms: peel, clip

fictional, relating to imaginative creation

She found she was more productive when writing *fictive* stories rather than autobiography.

synonyms: not genuine

PARE

verb (payr)

FILIBUSTER

verb (fihl ih buhs tuhr)

supreme, of chief importance

It's of *paramount* importance that we make it back to camp before the storm hits.

synonyms: primary, dominant

to use obstructionist tactics, especially prolonged speech making, in order to delay something

The congressman read names from the phonebook in an attempt to *filibuster* a pending bill.

synonyms: stall

PARAMOUNT

adj (paar uh mownt)

FITFUL

adj (fiht fuhl)

a model of excellence or perfection

She's the *paragon* of what a judge should be: honest, intelligent, and just.

synonyms: ideal, paradigm

intermittent, lacking steadiness; characterized by irregular bursts of activity

> Her *fitful* breathing became cause for concern, and eventually, she phoned the doctor.

synonyms: sporadic, periodic

PARAGON

noun (paar uh gahn)

FLIPPANT

adj (<u>flihp</u> uhnt)

an outstandingly clear or typical example

The new restaurant owner used the fast-food giant as a *paradigm* for expansion into new locales.

synonyms: model

marked by disrespectful lightheartedness or casualness

> Her *flippant* response was unacceptable and she was asked again to explain herself.

synonyms: pert, disrespectful

PARADIGM

noun (paar uh diem)

FLOUT

verb (flowt)

elaborate praise; formal hymn of praise

The director's *panegyric* for the donor who kept his charity going was heart-warming.

synonyms: compliment, homage

to scorn, to disregard with contempt

> The protestors *flouted* the committee's decision and hoped to sway public opinion.

synonyms: mock, sneer, spurn

PANEGYRIC

noun (paan uh geer ihk)

FODDER

noun (<u>fahd</u> uhr)

occurring over a wide geographic area and affecting a large portion of the population

Pandemic alarm spread throughout Colombia after the devastating earthquake.

synonyms: general, extensive

raw material, as for artistic creation; readily abundant ideas or images

The governor's hilarious blunder was good *fodder* for the comedian.

synonyms: material

PANDEMIC

adj (paan deh mihk)

FOREGO

verb (fohr goh)

flamboyance or dash in style and action

Leah has such *panache* when planning parties, even when they're last-minute affairs.

synonyms: flair

to precede, to go ahead of

Because of the risks of the expedition, the team leader made sure to *forego* the climbers.

PANACHE

noun (puh nahsh)

FORGO

verb (fohr <u>goh</u>)

pitifully small or worthless

Bernardo paid the ragged boy the *paltry* sum of 25 cents to carry his luggage all the way to the hotel.

synonyms: trifling, petty

to do without, to abstain from

As much as I wanted to *forgo* statistics, I knew it would serve me well in my field of study.

synonyms: pass on

PALTRY

adj (pawl tree)

FORMIDABLE

adj (<u>fohr</u> mih duh buhl) (fohr <u>mih</u> duh buhl)

capable of being touched or felt; easily perceived

The tension was *palpable* as I walked into the room.

synonyms: readily detected, tangible

fearsome, daunting; tending to inspire awe or wonder

The wrestler was not very big, but his skill and speed made him a *formidable* opponent.

synonyms: overpowering

PALPABLE

adj (paalp uh buhl)

an object or place having diverse layers or aspects beneath the surface

Years ago, paper was very expensive, so the practice was to write over previous words, creating a *palimpsest* of writing.

FORTITUDE

noun (fohr tih tood)

strength of mind that allows one to encounter adversity with courage

Months in the trenches exacted great *fortitude* of the soldiers.

synonyms: endurance, courage

PALIMPSEST

noun (paal ihmp sehst)

FORTUITOUS

adj (fohr <u>too</u> ih tuhs)

relating to a palace; magnificent

After living in a cramped studio apartment for years, Alicia thought the modest one bedroom looked downright *palatial.*

synonyms: grand, stately

by chance, especially by favorable chance

After a *fortuitous* run-in with an agent, Roxy won a recording contract.

synonyms: accidental

PALATIAL

adj (puh lay shuhl)

FRENETIC

adj (fruh <u>neht</u> ihk)

KAPLAN

a tribute, a song or expression of praise

He considered his newest painting a *paean* to his late wife.

frantic, frenzied

The employee's *frenetic* schedule left him little time to socialize.

synonyms: feverish

PAEAN

noun (pē uhn)

FULSOME

adj (<u>fool</u> suhm)

to remove from position by force; eject

After President Nixon so offensively lied to the country during Watergate, he was *ousted* from office.

synonyms: dismiss, evict

abundant; flattering in an insincere way

> The king's servant showered him with *fulsome* compliments in hopes of currying favor.

synonyms: insincere, saccharine

OUST

verb (owst)

FURLOUGH

noun (<u>fuhr</u> loh)

to exclude from a group by common consent

Feeling *ostracized* from her friends, Tabitha couldn't figure out what she had done.

synonyms: isolate, excommunicate

a leave of absence, especially granted to soldier or a prisoner

After seeing months of combat, the soldier received a much-deserved *furlough*.

synonyms: time off

OSTRACIZE

verb (ahs truh siez)

FURTIVE

adj (<u>fuhr</u> tihv)

to change into bone; to become hardened or set in a rigidly conventional pattern

The forensics expert ascertained the body's age based on the degree to which the facial structure had *ossified*.

sly, with hidden motives

> The *furtive* glances they exchanged made me suspect they were up to something.

synonyms: secret, surreptitious

OSSIFY

verb (ah sih fie)

to swing back and forth like a pendulum; to vary between opposing beliefs or feelings

The move meant a new house in a lovely neighborhood, but she missed her friends, so she *oscillated* between joy and sadness.

synonyms: fluctuate, vary

GALVANIZE

verb (<u>gaal</u> vuh niez)

to shock; to arouse awareness

> The closing down of another homeless shelter *galvanized* the activist group into taking political action.

synonyms: vitalize, energize

OSCILLATE

verb (ah sihl ayt)

GAMELY

adj (<u>gaym</u> lee)

having an irritable disposition, cantankerous

My first impression of the taxi driver was that he was *ornery*, but then he explained that he'd just had a bad day.

synonyms: disagreeable, unfriendly

spiritedly, bravely

> The park ranger *gamely* navigated the trail up the steepest face of the mountain.

synonyms: excitedly

ORNERY

adj (ohr nuh ree)

GAUCHE

adj (gohsh)

disgraceful, shameful

She wrote an *opprobrious* editorial in the newspaper about the critic who tore her new play to shreds.

synonyms: scornful

lacking social refinement

Snapping one's fingers to get the waiter's attention is considered *gauche*.

synonyms: tactless, simple

OPPROBRIOUS

adj (uh proh bree uhs)

GRANDILOQUENCE

noun (graan dihl uh kwuhns)

one who takes advantage of any opportunity to achieve an end, with little regard for principles

The *opportunist* wasted no time in stealing the idea and presenting it as his own.

synonyms: user, self-seeker

pompous talk; fancy but meaningless language

> The headmistress was notorious for her *grandiloquence* at the lectern and her ostentatious clothes.

synonyms: bravado, pretension

OPPORTUNIST

noun (ahp uhr too nihst)

GREGARIOUS

adj (greh <u>gayr</u> ee uhs)

to express an opinion

At the "Let's Chat Talk Show," the audience member *opined* that the guest was in the wrong.

synonyms: point out, voice

outgoing, sociable

Unlike her introverted friends, Susan was very *gregarious*.

synonyms: convivial, friendly

OPINE

verb (oh pīen)

GROTTO

noun (grah toh)

a burden, an obligation

Antonia was beginning to feel the *onus* of having to feed her friend's cat for the month.

synonyms: responsibility, hardship

a small cave

Alone on the island, Philoctetes sought shelter in a *grotto*.

synonyms: cavern, recess, burrow

ONUS

noun (ōh nuhs)

HARANGUE

verb (huh <u>raang</u>)

KAPLAN

a government in which a small group exercises supreme control

In an *oligarchy*, the few who rule are generally wealthier and have more status than the others.

synonym: small government

to give a long speech

> Maria's parents *harangued* her when she told them she'd spent her money on magic beans.

synonyms: lecture, reprimand

OLIGARCHY

noun (oh lih gaar kee)

HEDONIST

noun (<u>hee</u> duhn ihst)

relating to the sense of smell

Whenever she entered a candle store, her *olfactory* sense was awakened.

synonyms: fragrant, odorous

one who pursues pleasure as a goal

> Michelle, an admitted *hedonist*, lays on the couch eating cookies every Saturday.

synonyms: pleasure-seeker, glutton

OLFACTORY

adj (ohl faak tuh ree)

HEGEMONY

noun (hih jeh muh nee)

unreasonably persistent

The *obstinate* journalist would not reveal his source, and thus, was jailed for 30 days.

synonyms: stubborn, headstrong

the domination of one state or group over its allies

When Germany claimed *hegemony* over Russia, Stalin was outraged.

synonyms: power, authority

OBSTINATE

adj (ahb stih nuht)

HERETICAL

adj (huh reh tih kuhl)

to confuse, make obscure

Benny always *obfuscates* the discussion by bringing in irrelevant facts.

synonyms: shadow, complicate

departing from accepted beliefs or standards, oppositional

> At the onset of the Inquisition, the *heretical* priest was forced to flee the country.

synonyms: unorthodox

OBFUSCATE

verb (ahb fyoo skayt)

HIATUS

noun (hie ay tuhs)

stubbornly persistent, resistant to persuasion

The president was *obdurate* on the matter, and no amount of public protest could change his mind.

synonyms: inflexible, inexorable, adamant

a gap or interruption in space, time, or continuity

After a long *hiatus* in Greece, the philosophy professor returned to university.

synonyms: break

OBDURATE

adj (ahb duhr uht)

HISTRIONICS

noun (hihs tree <u>ahn</u> ihks)

new and not resembling anything formerly known

Piercing any part of the body other than the earlobes was *novel* in the 1950s, but now it is quite common.

synonyms: original, innovative

deliberate display of emotion for effect; exaggerated behavior calculated for effect

With such *histrionics*, she should really consider becoming an actress.

synonyms: melodrama, theatrics

NOVEL

adj (nah vuhl)

HUBRIS

noun (<u>hyoo</u> brihs)

a statement that does not follow logically from anything previously said

After the heated political debate, her comment about cake was a real *non sequitur.*

synonyms: illogical argument, off-topic comment

excessive pride or self-confidence

Nathan's *hubris* spurred him to do things that many considered insensitive.

sysnonyms: presumption, arrogance

NON SEQUITUR

noun (nahn sehk wih tuhr)

HUSBAND

verb (<u>huhz</u> buhnd)

a system of scientific names

In botany class, we learned the *nomenclature* used to identify different species of roses.

synonyms: classification, codification

to manage economically; to use sparingly

The cyclist paced herself at the start of the race, knowing that if she *husbanded* her resources she'd have the strength to break out of the pack later on.

synonyms: conserve

NOMENCLATURE

noun (nōh muhn klay chuhr)

HYPOCRITE

noun (hih puh kriht)

belief that traditional values and beliefs are unfounded and that existence is useless; belief that conditions in the social organization are so bad as to make destruction desirable

Robert's *nihilism* expressed itself in his lack of concern with the norms of moral society.

synonyms: skepticism, terrorism

one who puts on a false appearance of virtue; one who criticizes a flaw he in fact possesses

What a *hypocrite*: He criticizes those who wear fur but then he buys for himself a leather shearling coat.

synonyms: pretender, deceiver

NIHILISM

noun (nie hihl ihz uhm)

IGNOBLE

adj (ihg <u>noh</u> buhl)

a newborn child

The *neonate* was born prematurely so she's still in the hospital.

synonyms: baby, infant

having low moral standards, not noble in character; mean

> The photographer was paid a princely sum for the picture of the self-proclaimed ethicist in the *ignoble* act of pick-pocketing.

synonyms: lowly, vulgar

NEONATE

noun (nee uh nayt)

ILLUSORY

adj (ih loo suhr ee) (ih loos ree)

intensely wicked or vicous

Nefarious deeds are never far from an evil-doer's mind.

synonyms: malevolent, sinister

producing illusion, deceptive

The desert explorer was devastated to discover that the lake he thought he had seen was in fact *illusory*.

synonyms: false, imaginary

NEFARIOUS

adj (nih fahr ee uhs)

IMBIBE

verb (ihm bieb)

the practice of communicating with the dead in order to predict the future

The practice of *necromancy* supposes belief in survival of the soul after death.

synonyms: sorcery, black magic

to receive into the mind and take in

If I always attend class, I can *imbibe* as much knowledge as possible.

synonyms: absorb

NECROMANCY

noun (nehk ruh maan see)

IMPASSIVE

adj (ihm <u>paas</u> sihv)

vague, undefined

The candidate's *nebulous* plans to fight crime made many voters skeptical.

synonyms: hazy, unclear

absent of any external sign of emotion, expressionless

> Given his *impassive* expression, it was hard to tell whether he approved of my plan.

synonyms: apathetic, unemotional

NEBULOUS

adj (neh byoo luhs)

IMPERIOUS

adj (ihm <u>pihr</u> ee uhs)

lacking foresight, having a narrow view or long-range perspective

Not wanting to spend a lot of money up front, the *myopic* business owner would likely suffer the consequences later.

synonyms: short-sighted, unthinking

commanding, domineering; urgent

Though the king had been a kind leader, his daughter was *imperious* and demanding during her rule.

synonyms: authoritarian

MYOPIC

adj (mie ahp ihk) (mie oh pihk)

IMPERTURBABLE

adj (ihm puhr tuhr buh buhl)

the quality of being capable of change, in form or character; susceptibility of change

The actress lacked the *mutability* needed to perform in the improvisational play.

synonyms: inconstancy, variation

unshakably calm and steady

No matter how disruptive the children became, the babysitter remained *imperturbable.*

synonyms: cool, unflappable

MUTABILITY

noun (myoo tuh bihl uh tee)

IMPLACABLE

adj (ihm play kuh buhl) (ihm plaa kuh buhl)

a small particle, speck

Monica's eye watered, irritated by a *mote* of dust.

synonyms: bit, shred

inflexible; not capable of being changed or pacified

The *implacable* teasing was hard for the child to take.

synonyms: merciless, relentless

MOTE

noun (moht)

IMPORTUNATE

adj (ihm pohr chuh niht)

gloomy, sullen

After hearing that the internship had been given to someone else, Lenny was *morose* for days.

synonyms: pessimistic, dour

troublesomely urgent; extremely persistent in request or demand

Her *importunate* appeal for a job caused me to grant her an interview.

synonyms: insistent, obstinate

MOROSE

adj (muh rohs) (maw rohs)

IMPRECATION

noun (ihm prih kay shuhn)

fixed customs or manners; moral attitudes

In keeping with the *mores* of ancient Roman society, Nero held a celebration every weekend.

synonyms: conventions, practices

a curse

> Spouting violent *imprecations*, Hank searched for the person who had vandalized his truck.

synonyms: damnation

MORES

noun (mawr ayz)

IMPUDENT

adj (ihm pyuh duhnt)

biting and caustic in manner and style

Roald Dahl's stories are *mordant* alternatives to bland kids' stories.

synonyms: scathing, hurtful

marked by cocky boldness or disregard for others

> Considering the judge had been lenient in her sentence, it was *impudent* of the defendant to refer to her by her first name.

synonyms: arrogant, insolent

MORDANT

adj (mohr dnt)

IMPUGN

verb (ihm pyoon)

to soothe in temper or disposition

A small raise and increased break time *mollified* the unhappy staff, at least for the moment.

synonyms: pacify, appease

to call into question; to attack verbally

"How dare you *impugn* my motives?" protested the lawyer, on being accused of ambulance chasing.

synonyms: challenge, dispute

MOLLIFY

verb (mahl uh fie)

IMPUTE

verb (ihm pyoot)

a small portion, limited quantity

I expect at least a *modicum* of assistance from you on the day of the party.

synonyms: crumb, iota

to lay the responsibility or blame for, often unjustly

> It seemed unfair to *impute* the accident on me, especially since they were the ones who ran the red light.

synonyms: ascribe, attribute, pin on

MODICUM

noun (mahd ih kuhm)

INCANDESCENT

adj (ihn kuhn dehs uhnt)

to make less severe, make milder

A judge may *mitigate* a sentence if it's decided that the crime was committed out of necessity.

synonyms: relieve, alleviate

shining brightly

The *incandescent* glow of the moon made it a night I'll never forget.

synonyms: brilliant, radiant

MITIGATE

verb (miht ih gayt)

INCARNADINE

adj (ihn kaar nuh dien) (ihn kaar nuh dihn)

a written note or letter

Priscilla spent hours composing a romantic *missive* for Elvis.

synonyms: message

red, especially blood red

The *incarnadine* lipstick she wore made her look much older than she was.

synonyms: sanguine

MISSIVE

noun (mihs ihv)

INCHOATE

adj (ihn koh iht)

an error in naming a person or place

Iceland is a *misnomer* since it isn't really icy; the name means "island."

synonyms: error, misapplication

being only partly in existence; imperfectly formed

For every page of the crisp writing that made it into the final book, Jessie has 10 pages of *inchoate* rambling that made up the first draft.

synonyms: formless, undefined

MISNOMER

noun (mihs noh muhr)

INCIPIENT

adj (ihn <u>sihp</u> ee uhnt)

a person who hates or distrusts mankind

Scrooge was such a *misanthrope* that even the sight of children singing made him angry.

synonyms: curmudgeon

beginning to exist or appear; in an initial stage

> The *incipient* idea seemed brilliant, but they knew it needed much more development.

synonyms: developing, basic

MISANTHROPE

noun (mihs uhn throhp)

INCORRIGIBLE

adj (ihn <u>kohr</u> ih juh buhl)

synonyms: background

The *milieu* at the club wasn't one I was comfortable with, so I left right away.

the physical or social setting in which something occurs or develops, environment

incapable of being corrected or changed; difficult to control or manage

> "You're *incorrigible*," yelled the frustrated mother to her son, in the middle of his third tantrum of the day.

synonyms: delinquent, unfixable

MILIEU

noun (mihl yoo)

INCREDULOUS

adj (ihn krehj uh luhs)

a small scale representation of a larger system

This department is in fact a *microcosm* of the entire corporation.

unwilling to accept what is said to be true, skeptical

> The Lasky children were *incredulous* when their parents sat them down and told them the facts of life.

synonyms: doubtful, disbelieving

MICROCOSM

noun (mie kruh kahz uhm)

INDOMITABLE

adj (ihn dahm ih tuh buhl)

having a smooth, rich flow

She was so talented that her *mellifluous* flute playing transported me to another world.

synonyms: melodious

incapable of being conquered

> Climbing Mount Everest would seem an *indomitable* task, but it has been done many times.

synonyms: insurmountable

MELLIFLUOUS

adj (muh lihf loo uhs)

INGRATIATE

verb (ihn gray shee ayt)

synonyms: egoism, self-centeredness

Many of the Roman emperors suffered from severe *megalomania.*

obsession with great or grandiose performance

to gain favor with another by deliberate effort, to seek to please somebody so as to gain an advantage

The new intern tried to *ingratiate* herself with the managers so that they might consider her for a future job.

synonyms: flatter, curry favor

MEGALOMANIA

noun (mehg uh loh may nee uh)

sickeningly sentimental

The poet hoped to charm his girlfriend with his flowery poem, but its *mawkish* tone sickened her instead.

synonyms: maudlin

INHERENT

adj (ihn <u>hehr</u> ehnt)

involved essential character of something, built-in, inborn

> The class was dazzled by the experiment and as a result more likely to remember the *inherent* scientific principle.

synonyms: intrinsic

MAWKISH

adj (maw kihsh)

INQUEST

noun (<u>ihn</u> kwehst)

an independent individual who does not go along with a group

The senator was a *maverick* who was willing to vote against his own party's position.

synonyms: nonconformist

an investigation, an inquiry

The police chief ordered an *inquest* to determine what went wrong.

MAVERICK

noun (maav rihk) (maav uh rihk)

INSENSATE

adj (ihn sehn sayt) (ihn sehn siht)

one who enjoys being subjected to pain or humiliation

Only a *masochist* would volunteer to take on this nightmarish project.

lacking sensibility and understanding, foolish

The shock of the accident left him *insensate*, but after some time, the numbness subsided and he was able to tell the officer what had happened.

synonyms: unfeeling, callous

MASOCHIST

noun (maas uhk ihst)

artificial or stilted in character

The portrait is an example of the *mannered* style that was favored in that era.

synonyms: affected, unnatural

INSOLENT

adj (<u>ihn</u> suh luhnt)

insultingly arrogant, overbearing

> After having spoken with three *insolent* customer service representatives, Shelly was relieved when the fourth one sympathized with her complaint.

synonyms: offensive, rude

MANNERED

adj (maan uhrd)

INSULAR

adj (<u>ihn</u> suh luhr) (<u>ihn</u> syuh luhr)

KAPLAN

easily influenced or shaped, capable of being altered by outside forces

The welder heated the metal before shaping it because the heat made it malleable.

synonyms: adaptable, pliable

characteristic of an isolated people, especially having a narrow viewpoint

> It was a shock for Kendra to go from her small high school, with her *insular* group of friends, to a huge college with students from all over the country.

synonyms: provincial, narrow-minded

MALLEABLE

adj (maal ee uh buhl)

INSUPERABLE

adj (ihn soo puhr uh buhl)

wrongdoing or misconduct, especially by a public official

Not only was the deputy's *malfeasance* humiliating, it also spelled the end of his career.

synonyms: corruption, fraud

incapable of being surmounted or overcome

> *Insuperable* as though our problems may seem, I'm confident we'll come out ahead.

synonyms: unconquerable

MALFEASANCE

noun (mal fee zuhns)

INTER

verb (ihn <u>tuhr</u>)

exhibiting ill will; wishing harm to others

The *malevolent* gossiper spread false rumors with frequency.

synonyms: malicious, hateful

to bury

After giving the masses one last chance to pay their respects, the leader's body was *interred*.

synonym: entomb

MALEVOLENT

adj (muh lehv uh luhnt)

INTERLOCUTOR

noun (ihn tuhr lahk yuh tuhr)

a curse, a wish of evil upon another

The frog prince looked for a princess to kiss him and put an end to the witch's *malediction.*

synonyms: damnation, commination

ones who takes part in conversation

> Though always the *interlocutor*, the professor actually preferred that his students guide the class discussion.

MALEDICTION

noun (maal ih dihk shun)

INTERNECINE

adj (ihn tuhr nehs een)

KAPLAN

the accidental, often comical, use of a word which resembles the one intended, but has a different, often contradictory meaning

Everybody laughed at the *malapropism* when instead of saying "public broadcasting" the announcer said "public boredcasting."

synonyms: misstatement

mutually destructive; equally devastating to both sides

Though it looked as though there was a victor, the *internecine* battle benefited no one.

KAPLAN

MALAPROPISM

noun (maal uh prahp ihz uhm)

INTERREGNUM

noun (ihn tuhr <u>rehg</u> nuhm)

a feeling of unease or depression

During his presidency, Jimmy Carter spoke of a "national *malaise*" and was subsequently criticized for being too negative.

synonyms: discomfort, unhappiness

a temporary halting of the usual operations of government or control

> The new king began his reign by restoring order that the lawless *interregnum* had destroyed.

synonyms: hiatus, interruption

MALAISE

noun (maa layz)

INTIMATION

noun (ihn tuh <u>may</u> shuhn)

the whole universe; a large-scale reflection of a part of the great world

Some scientists focus on a particular aspect of space, while others study the entire *macrocosm* and how its parts relate to one another.

synonyms: cosmos

a subtle and indirect hint

Abby chose to ignore Babu's *intimation* that she wasn't as good a swimmer as she claimed.

synonyms: suggestion, insinuation

MACROCOSM

noun (maak roh kahz uhm)

INTRACTABLE

adj (ihn traak tuh buhl)

having death as a subject; dwelling on the gruesome

Martin enjoyed *macabre* tales about werewolves and vampires.

synonyms: ghastly, grim

not easily managed or manipulated

Intractable for hours, the wild horse eventually allowed the rider to mount.

synonyms: stubborn, unruly

MACABRE

adj (muh kaa bruh) (muh kaa buhr)

INTRANSIGENT

adj (ihn traan suh juhnt) (ihn traan zuh juhnt)

talkative

She was naturally *loquacious*, which was always a challenge when she was in a library or movie theater.

synonyms: chatty

uncompromising, refusing to abandon an extreme position

His *intransigent* positions on social issues cost him the election.

synonyms: obstinate, unyielding

LOQUACIOUS

adj (loh kway shuhs)

INTREPID

adj (ihn <u>trehp</u> ihd)

moving and bending with ease; marked by effortless grace

The dancer's *lithe* movements proved her to be a rising star in the ballet corps.

synonyms: flexible, limber

fearless, resolutely courageous

Despite freezing winds, the *intrepid* hiker completed his ascent.

synonyms: brave

LITHE

adj (lie*th*)

INUNDATE

verb (<u>ihn</u> uhn dayt)

flexible, capable of being shaped

After years of doing so much yoga, the elderly man was remarkably *limber*.

synonyms: agile, nimble

to cover with a flood; to overwhelm as if with a flood

> The box office was *inundated* with requests for tickets to the award-winning play.

synonyms: swamp, drown

LIMBER

adj (lihm buhr)

INVETERATE

adj (ihn veht uhr iht)

a very small person or thing

Next to her Amazonian roommate, the girl appeared to be *lilliputian.*

synonyms: diminutive, small

firmly established, especially with respect to a habit or attitude

An *inveterate* risk-taker, Lori tried her luck at bungee-jumping.

synonyms: habitual, chronic

LILLIPUTIAN

noun (lihl ee pyoo shun)

IRASCIBLE

adj (ih raas uh buhl)

immoral; unrestrained by society

Religious citizens were outraged by the *licentious* exploits of the free-spirited artists living in town.

synonyms: wanton, lewd

easily angered, hot-tempered

> One of the most *irascible* barbarians of all time, Attila the Hun ravaged much of Europe during his time.

synonyms: irritable, crabby

LICENTIOUS

adj (lei sehn shuhs)

IRONIC

adj (ie rahn ihk)

KAPLAN

a free thinker, usually used disparagingly; one without moral restraint

The *libertine* took pleasure in gambling away his family's money.

synonyms: hedonist

poignantly contrary or incongruous to what was expected

It was *ironic* to learn that shy Wendy from high school grew up to be the loud-mouth host of the daily talk show.

LIBERTINE

noun (lihb uhr teen)

IRREVERENT

adj (ih rehv uhr uhnt)

one who advocates individual rights and free will

The *libertarian* was always at odds with the conservatives.

disrespectful in a gentle or humorous way

Kevin's *irreverent* attitude toward the principal annoyed the teacher but amused the other children.

synonyms: cheeky, satiric

LIBERTARIAN

noun (lih buhr tehr ee uhn)

ITINERANT

adj (ie <u>tihn</u> uhr uhnt)

a dictionary; a stock of terms pertaining to a particular subject or vocabulary

The author coined the term Gen-X, which has since entered the *lexicon*.

synonyms: dictionary, vocabulary

wandering from place to place; unsettled

The *itinerant* tomcat came back to the Johansson homestead every two months.

synonyms: nomadic, vagrant

LEXICON

noun (lehk sih kahn)

JETTISON

verb (jeht ih zuhn) (jeht ih suhn)

an inappropriate lack of seriousness, overly casual

The joke added needed *levity* to the otherwise serious meeting.

synonyms: amusement, humor

to discard, to get rid of as unnecessary or encumbering

> The sinking ship *jettisoned* its cargo in a desperate attempt to reduce its weight.

synonyms: eject, dump

LEVITY

noun (leh vih tee)

JOCULAR

adj (jahk yuh luhr)

---

lewd, lustful

The school board censored the movie because of its portrayal of the *lecherous* criminal.

synonyms: lascivious, promiscuous

playful, humorous

The *jocular* old man entertained his grandchildren for hours.

synonyms: comical, amusing

LECHEROUS

adj (lehch uh ruhs)

KAPLAN

JUNTA

noun (hoon tuh) (juhn tuh)

not rigid, loose; negligent

Because our delivery boy is *lax*, the newspaper often arrives sopping wet.

synonyms: careless, imprecise

a small governing body, especially after a revolutionary seizure of power

Only one member of the *junta* was satisfactory enough to be elected once the new government was established.

synonyms: council

LAX

adj (laaks)

KISMET

noun (kihz meht) (kihz miht)

deserving of praise

Kristin's dedication is *laudable*, but she doesn't have the necessary skills to be a good paralegal.

synonyms: commendable, admirable

destiny, fate

When Eve found out that Garret also played the harmonica, she knew their meeting was *kismet*.

LAUDABLE

adj (law duh buhl)

LAMPOON

verb (laam <u>poon</u>)

generous giving (as of money) to others who may seem inferior

She'd always relied on her parent's *largess*, but after graduation, she had to get a job.

synonyms: generosity, benevolence

to ridicule with satire

The mayor hated being *lampooned* by the press for his efforts to improve people's politeness.

synonyms: tease, mock, parody

LARGESS

noun (laar jehs)

SAT ROOT LIST

A, AN—not, without

AB, A—from, away, apart

AC, ACR—sharp, sour

AD, A—to, towards

ALI, ALTR—another

AM, AMI—love

AMBI, AMPHI—both

AMBL, AMBUL—walk

ANIM—mind, spirit, breath

ANN, ENN—year

ANTE, ANT—before

ANTHROP—human

ANTI, ANT—against, opposite

AUD—hear

AUTO—self

BELLI, BELL—war

BENE, BEN—good

BI—two

BIBLIO—book

BIO—life

BURS—money, purse

CAD, CAS, CID—happen, fall

CAP, CIP—head

CARN—flesh

CAP, CAPT, CEPT, CIP—take, hold, seize

CED, CESS—yield, go

CHROM—color

CHRON—time

CIDE—murder

CIRCUM—around

CLIN, CLIV—slope

CLUD, CLUS, CLAUS, CLOIS—shut, close

CO, COM, CON—with, together

COGN, GNO—know

CONTRA—against

CORP—body

COSMO, COSM—world

CRAC, CRAT—rule, power

CRED—trust, believe

CRESC, CRET—grow

CULP—blame, fault

CURR, CURS—run

DE—down, out, apart

DEC—ten, tenth

DEMO, DEM—people

DI, DIURN—day

DIA—across

DIC, DICT—speak

DIS, DIF, DI—not, apart, away
DOC, DOCT—teach
DOL—pain
DUC, DUCT—lead
EGO—self
EN, EM—in, into
ERR—wander
EU—well, good
EX, E—out, out of
FAC, FIC, FECT, FY, FEA—make, do
FAL, FALS—deceive
FERV—boil
FID—faith, trust
FLU, FLUX—flow
FORE—before
FRAG, FRAC—break
FUS—pour
GEN—birth, class, kin
GRAD, GRESS—step
GRAPH, GRAM—writing
GRAT—pleasing
GRAV, GRIEV—heavy
GREG—crowd, flock
HABIT, HIBIT—have, hold
HAP—by chance
HELIO, HELI—sun
HETERO—other
HOL—whole
HOMO—same
HOMO—man
HYDR—water
HYPER—too much, excess
HYPO—too little, under
IN, IG, IL, IM, IR—not
IN, IL, IM, IR—in, on, into
INTER—between, among
INTRA, INTR—within
IT, ITER—between, among
JECT, JET—throw
JOUR—day
JUD—judge
JUNCT, JUG—join
JUR—swear, law
LAT—side
LAV, LAU, LU—wash
LEG, LEC, LEX—read, speak
LEV—light
LIBER—free
LIG, LECT—choose, gather
LIG, LI, LY—bind
LING, LANG—tongue

LITER—letter

LITH—stone

LOQU, LOC, LOG—speech, thought

LUC, LUM—light

LUD, LUS—play

MACRO—great

MAG, MAJ, MAS, MAX—great

MAL—bad

MAN—hand

MAR—sea

MATER, MATR—mother

MEDI—middle

MEGA—great

MEM, MEN—remember

METER, METR, MENS—measure

MICRO—small

MIS—wrong, bad, hate

MIT, MISS—send

MOLL—soft

MON, MONIT—warn

MONO—one

MOR—custom, manner

MOR, MORT—dead

MORPH—shape

MOV, MOT, MOB, MOM—move

MUT—change

NAT, NASC—born

NAU, NAV—ship, sailor

NEG—not, deny

NEO—new

NIHIL—none, nothing

NOM, NYM—name

NOX, NIC, NEC, NOC—harm

NOV—new

NUMER—number

OB—against

OMNI—all

ONER—burden

OPER—work

PAC—peace

PALP—feel

PAN—all

PATER, PATR—father

PATH, PASS—feel, suffer

PEC—money

PED, POD—foot

PEL, PULS—drive

PEN—almost

PEND, PENS—hang

PER—through, by, for, throughout

PER—against, destruction

PERI—around
PET—seek, go towards
PHIL—love
PHOB—fear
PHON—sound
PLAC—calm, please
PON, POS—put, place
PORT—carry
POT—drink
POT—power
PRE—before
PRIM, PRI—first
PRO—ahead, forth
PROTO—first
PROX, PROP—near
PSEUDO—false
PYR—fire

QUAD, QUAR, QUAT—four
QUES, QUER, QUIS, QUIR—question
QUIE—quiet
QUINT, QUIN—five
RADI, RAMI—branch
RECT, REG—straight, rule
REG—king, rule
RETRO—backward
RID, RIS—laugh
ROG—ask
RUD—rough, crude
RUPT—break
SACR, SANCT—holy
SCRIB, SCRIPT, SCRIV—write
SE—apart, away
SEC, SECT, SEG—cut
SED, SID—sit

SEM—seed, sow
SEN—old
SENT, SENS—feel, think
SEQU, SECU—follow
SIM, SEM—similar, same
SIGN—mark, sign
SIN—curve
SOL—sun
SOL—alone
SOMN—sleep
SON—sound
SOPH—wisdom
SPEC, SPIC—see, look
SPER—hope
SPERS, SPAR—scatter
SPIR—breathe
STRICT, STRING—bind

STRUCT, STRU—build

SUB—under

SUMM—highest

SUPER, SUR—above

SURGE, SURRECT—rise

SYN, SYM—together

TACIT, TIC—silent

TACT, TAG, TANG—touch

TEN, TIN, TAIN—hold, twist

TEND, TENS, TENT—stretch

TERM—end

TERR—earth, land

TEST—witness

THE—god

THERM—heat

TIM—fear, frightened

TOP—place

TORT—twist

TORP—stiff, numb

TOX—poison

TRACT—draw

TRANS—across, over, through, beyond

TREM, TREP—shake

TURB—shake

UMBR—shadow

UNI, UN— one

URB—city

VAC—empty

VAL, VAIL—value, strength

VEN, VENT—come

VER—true

VERB—word

VERT, VERS—turn

VICT, VINC—conquer

VID, VIS—see

VIL—base, mean

VIV, VIT—life

VOC, VOK, VOW—call, voice

VOL—wish

VOLV, VOLUT—turn, roll

VOR—eat